Reversible Digital Watermarking

Theory and Practices

Synthesis Lectures on Information Security, Privacy, and Trust

Editor
Elisa Bertino, *Purdue University*
Ravi Sandhu, *University of Texas, San Antonio*

The Synthesis Lectures Series on Information Security, Privacy, and Trust publishes 50- to 100-page publications on topics pertaining to all aspects of the theory and practice of Information Security, Privacy, and Trust. The scope largely follows the purview of premier computer security research journals such as ACM *Transactions on Information and System Security,* IEEE *Transactions on Dependable and Secure Computing* and *Journal of Cryptology,* and premier research conferences such as ACM CCS, ACM SACMAT, ACM AsiaCCS, ACM CODASPY, IEEE Security and Privacy, IEEE Computer Security Foundations, ACSAC, ESORICS, Crypto, EuroCrypt and AsiaCrypt. In addition to the research topics typically covered in such journals and conferences, the series also solicits lectures on legal, policy, social, business, and economic issues addressed to a technical audience of scientists and engineers. Lectures on significant industry developments by leading practitioners are also solicited.

Reversible Digital Watermarking: Theory and Practices
Ruchira Naskar and Rajat Subhra Chakraborty

ISBN: 978-3-031-01214-3   print
ISBN: 978-3-031-02342-2   ebook

DOI: 10.1007/978-3-031-02342-2

A Publication in the Springer series
SYNTHESIS LECTURES ON INFORMATION SECURITY, PRIVACY, AND TRUST
Series ISSN: 1945-9742 print   1945-9750 ebook

Lecture #10
Series Editors: Elisa Bertino, *Purdue University,* and Ravi Sandhu, *University of Texas, San Antonio*

First Edition
10 9 8 7 6 5 4 3 2 1

Reversible Digital Watermarking

Theory and Practices

Ruchira Naskar
National Institute of Technology Rourkela

Rajat Subhra Chakraborty
Indian Institute of Technology Kharagpur

SYNTHESIS LECTURES ON INFORMATION SECURITY, PRIVACY, AND TRUST #10

ABSTRACT

Digital Watermarking is the art and science of embedding information in existing digital content for Digital Rights Management (DRM) and authentication. *Reversible watermarking* is a class of (fragile) digital watermarking that not only authenticates multimedia data content, but also helps to maintain perfect integrity of the original multimedia "cover data." In non-reversible watermarking schemes, after embedding and extraction of the watermark, the cover data undergoes some distortions, although perceptually negligible in most cases. In contrast, in reversible watermarking, zero-distortion of the cover data is achieved, that is the cover data is guaranteed to be restored bit-by-bit. Such a feature is desirable when highly sensitive data is watermarked, e.g., in military, medical and legal imaging applications. This work deals with development, analysis and evaluation of state-of-the-art reversible watermarking techniques for digital images. In this work we establish the motivation for research on reversible watermarking using a couple of case studies with medical and military images. We present a detailed review of the state-of-the-art research in this field. We investigate the various subclasses of reversible watermarking algorithms, their operating principles and computational complexities. Along with this, to give the readers an idea about the detailed working of a reversible watermarking scheme, we present a prediction-based reversible watermarking technique, recently published by us. We discuss the major issues and challenges behind implementation of reversible watermarking techniques, and recently proposed solutions for them. Finally, we provide an overview of some open problems and scope of work for future researchers in this area.

KEYWORDS

digital rights management, digital watermarking, lossless data hiding, multimedia data, reversibility

Dedicated to our families

Contents

List of Figures

List of Tables

List of Algorithms

Preface

This book addresses *Digital Rights Management* issues related to multimedia data, specifically digital images transmitted over inherently insecure communication networks such as the Internet. *Digital Rights Management* includes copyright protection, copy prevention, broadcast monitoring, etc. With the wide global proliferation of the Internet at present, *Digital Rights Management* has become a critical issue for safety and security of multimedia data.

In this book we broadly discuss *Digital Watermarking* as a technique of *Digital Rights Management*. More specifically, we focus on watermarking of highly security sensitive digital images, where information loss due to the embedding step of digital watermarking is a critical safety and security concern. We discuss the state-of-the-art principles and practices of *Lossless Watermarking* or *Reversible Watermarking*, which are widely used in industries dealing with such sensitive data, for example, the medical, military or legal industries.

In Chapter 1, we present a broad overview of *Digital Watermarking* with emphasis on importance of *Reversible Watermarking*. In Chapter 2, we present two case studies carried out on medical and military images respectively, to establish the need behind research on *Reversible Watermarking*. An extensive literature survey of state-of-the-art reversible watermarking techniques is presented in Chapter 3, along with detailed discussion on the methodology of the most recent techniques developed.

Chapter 4 presents in detail the workings of a recently developed reversible watermarking technique. In Chapter 5 we address the major issues and challenges faced by developers of reversible watermarking schemes and present some solutions to those challenges. A "tamper detection and localization" technology for reversible watermarking schemes is presented in Chapter 6. Finally, we conclude and discuss the future research directions in Chapter 7.

ACKNOWLEDGMENTS

We sincerely express our deepest gratitude toward all members of the *Secured Embedded Architecture Laboratory* of the Department of Computer Science and Engineering, IIT Kharagpur, for their cooperation and best wishes. We would also like to thank our respective family members for their patience and understanding while the book was being written.

CHAPTER 1

Introduction

1.1 DIGITAL WATERMARKING

Digital watermarking [1] is the act of hiding information in multimedia data, for the purposes of content protection or authentication. In ordinary digital watermarking, the secret information—the *watermark*—is embedded into the multimedia data (*cover data*) in such a way that distortion of the cover data due to watermarking is almost negligible perceptually. General application domains of digital watermarking include broadcast monitoring, owner identification, transaction tracking, content authentication, copy control and many more. The recent advances in the reach of internet on a global scale has led to the widespread distribution of digital content over the internet. This progress helps various businesses to be able to reach more audience, but at the same time, also creates the possibility of illegal copying and distribution of the content. Therefore, digital media suppliers need technologies that are backed by legislation to secure digital media from illegal usage [2]. "Digital Rights Management" (DRM) is a collection of technologies that enforces the usage of digital media in compliance with the established privileges and thus helps in the protection of digital media [3]. *Digital watermarking*, which is one of the main tools in the repertoire of DRM, is widely used to protect the copyright of digital content.

Watermarking Trade-offs

High-performance digital watermarking is a challenging research area where there is no "silver bullet" technique that can satisfy all the watermarking requirements. As illustrated in Fig. 1.1, the three mutually exclusive factors, which are the parameters to evaluate the performance of any digital watermarking scheme, are as follows.

Quality. Perceptual quality of the watermarked data. The lower the distortion of the cover data after watermarking, the higher its quality.

Capacity. Maximum size (number of symbols or bits) of watermark that may be embedded into a cover data by the watermarking scheme.

Robustness. The ability of the watermarked data to withstand any kind of modification. The more robust a watermarking scheme is, the lower the probability of a modification of the watermarked data being detected at the receiver side.

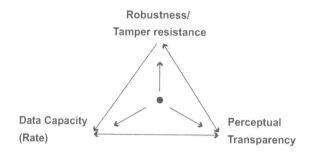

FIGURE 1.1: Classical trade-offs in watermarking.

Unfortunately, trying to improve one of these factors for a particular watermarking scheme usually deteriorates one or both of the others. For example, the more robust a watermarking scheme is, the greater its capability to withstand any kind of modification or tampering, without being detected by the receiver. On the contrary, any modification or tampering going undetected denotes nothing but reduction of authentication capability (capability to maintain data integrity) of the algorithm. In other words, when robustness is improved, it hampers authentication capabilities of the watermarking algorithm. Similarly, when one tries to improve the embedding capacity of a watermarking scheme, it deteriorates the perceptual quality of the cover data. So, one needs to attain a trade-off between all three parameters while designing a watermarking scheme, to consider it acceptable for practical purposes. In other words, the performance of an ideal watermarking scheme must be such that it can be placed somewhere within the triangle shown in Fig. 1.1. For example, if required, a watermarking scheme should be capable of providing higher embedding capacity, but still continue to give acceptable robustness and perceptual quality of the watermarked image.

1.2   FRAGILE AND ROBUST WATERMARKING TECHNIQUES

Fragile watermarking [1] is mainly used for content authentication of multimedia data. In fragile watermarking algorithms, the watermark is generally a secure keyed hash of the entire cover signal. Even a minimal modification of the cover multimedia data (e.g. a single bit in the extreme case) by an adversary destroys a fragile watermark, and consequently causes authentication failure at the receiver side. In other words, a fragile watermark is desirably destroyed and is rendered undetectable, even in the case of minimal modification of the watermarked cover data.

On the contrary, *robust watermarking* [1] techniques are developed to resist any kind of attack, modification or tampering of the cover data by an adversary. Robust watermarking algorithms are designed to achieve the maximum possible robustness against any intentional or unintentional modification of the watermarked data. The most common forms of modifications that robust watermarks are designed to resist are as follows:

Geometric distortions , such as rotation, scaling, translation, skew, transformation, cropping, etc.

Temporal distortions , such as delay and temporal scaling).

Valumetric distortions , such as additive noise, amplitude changes, linear filtering, quantization, lossy compression, etc.

1.3 REVERSIBLE DIGITAL WATERMARKING

In industries dealing with highly sensitive data such as the medical, military or legal industries, even the minimal data distortions are difficult to be tolerated, even if not perceptually significant. In such domains, cover information is extremely sensitive and recovery of the original cover information in an unaltered form is of utmost importance. In such cases, *reversible watermarking* algorithms have been found useful where by the very nature of the watermarking algorithm, the original cover data content, can be retrieved exactly with zero-distortion. Reversible watermarking algorithms belong to the class of fragile watermarking algorithms. In state-of-the-art reversible watermarking algorithms [4, 5, 6, 7, 14, 20], the watermark is generally a secure hash of the cover image, which is generated by using any well-known cryptographic hash algorithm such as MD5 or SHA. At the receiver side, the watermark is extracted and the hash of the restored cover image is computed. The restored cover data is authenticated and accepted at the receiver end, only if the watermark and the computed hash match.

To authenticate digital multimedia data, the first idea that comes to one's mind is to turn to cryptographic hash functions. What is the need of watermarking in spite of the presence of highly efficient cryptographic techniques? In cryptography, the hash of the cover data to be authenticated is computed by using a hash function over the cover data. The hash message is now transmitted as separate information to the receiver, along with the cover data. Such techniques are suitable to protect digital data on transit, and are vulnerable to interception by an adversary, paving the path to subsequent man-in-the-middle attack. For digital multimedia data such as images, audio, video, etc., which are used on a regular basis by large masses of common people, protecting it once while transmission is not sufficient. In such cases, the hash needs to be kept embedded into the cover data for copyright control, copy protection, broadcast monitoring and similar purposes as discussed in Section 1.1. By digital watermarking, the watermarked data may be used widely without the need to maintain (store or transmit) any additional information. For specialized users having additional rights, the watermark may be extracted (and cover data restored in case of reversible watermarking), for authenticating and validating data integrity. Those special users are provided with keys to achieve

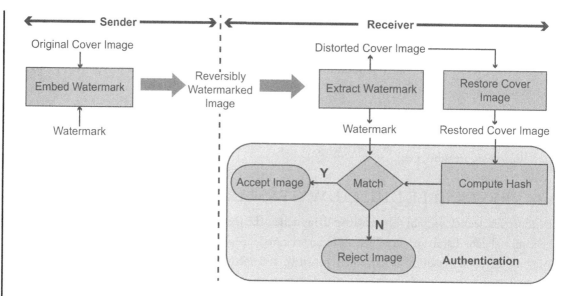

FIGURE 1.2: Reversible watermarking.

the above goals. In case of reversible watermarking, the key refers the combination of two bitstrings: the hash key (since reversible watermarking algorithms use keyed hash functions to generate the watermark) and the key used by the embedder to select the locations within the cover data where the watermark symbols are kept embedded.

The last decade has seen rapid growth of research interest in the field of reversible watermarking of multimedia data. Reversible watermarking is a technique used for authentication of digital multimedia data as well as distortion-free recovery of the original data contents after authentication. The primary goal of reversible watermarking is to maintain perfect integrity of the original content after watermark extraction. Among several reversible watermarking schemes that have been proposed until now by researchers, an overwhelming majority have been proposed for digital images. *Reversible watermarking* not only provides the protection of the cover signal (such as implementation of *Digital Rights Management* and other applications of any general digital watermarking, in addition to authentication), but also can restore the original cover signal from its watermarked version; and this restoration is 100% distortion-free. The extracted watermark can now be used to authenticate the restored cover signal. A generic reversible watermarking technique for digital multimedia data is depicted in Fig. 1.2.

A major challenge in reversible watermarking schemes is to restore the cover data back to its original form, after watermark extraction. Conventionally, reversible watermarking schemes implement cover data recovery by the use of *cover retrieval information* (see Fig. 1.2). Reversible watermarking techniques embed this *cover retrieval information* into the cover data, in addition to the watermark. Note here that, similar to any general (non-reversible) watermarking technique, in reversible watermarking algorithms embedding capacity refers to the capacity of embedding only pure watermark bits (not including the additional information) as well.

1.3.1 IMPORTANCE OF REVERSIBLE WATERMARKING

An example from the medical industry will illustrate the need of reversible watermarking clearly. Personal *Electronic Patient Records* (EPRs) are extremely important medical and legal documents, used by professionals such as doctors, clinical researchers and insurance companies. Often, EPRs are kept embedded into medical multimedia data (such as radiographs, urograms, mammograms etc.) of the patient concerned in the form of a digital watermark. If lossy watermarking techniques are adopted for the embedding, this causes some distortion of the cover data during embedding. Moreover, patient records change over time, and this phenomenon requires the embedded EPRs to be updated from time to time. Repeated extraction and embedding of EPRs in order to update them, using lossy watermarking techniques, causes the distortion of the cover data to accumulate. Since such accumulation of distortion might adversely affect the quality of the medical image, it becomes difficult to make the correct diagnosis. This situation is undesirable and can be improved by the use of reversible watermarking. In Chapter 2, we present a case study on medical images to demonstrate the efficiency of reversible watermarking, while dealing with security and integrity sensitive data, as compare to non-reversible watermarking.

CHAPTER 2

Motivational Case Studies

In this chapter we establish the motivation behind research on the topic of reversible digital water-marking through two case studies carried out on medical and military images (the major application domains of reversible watermarking). We show that the adoption of reversible watermarking tech-niques prevents deterioration of diagnosis accuracy (for medical images), and causes a lower residual error rate when images are communicated over a highly noisy channel (for military images).

2.1 INVESTIGATING THE EFFECTS OF DRM PRACTICES ON MEDICAL IMAGES

Telemedicine [29] is the technology and practice of electronic transmission of medical images, for the purpose of interpretation of those images by physicians, clinical experts, as well as medical researchers situated at a remote location. Pathological patient imaging, radiological patient imaging and nuclear patient imaging are some of the significant medical imaging techniques contributing to telemedicine. In telemedicine, the medical images of a patient might be transmitted across the world, often over public communication infrastructure such as the internet. Maintenance of security and confidentiality of medical information is of utmost priority [30], often enforced by law in many countries globally. Unfortunately, due to the above-mentioned frequent transmission of medical images in large numbers over potentially insecure communication channels, concerns about lapses in security and privacy have arisen in the medical industry. Therefore, with the advent of telemedicine, *Digital Rights Management* (DRM) of medical images has become a necessity in the present day medical industry. However, sometimes the acts of DRM, specifically watermarking, causes some information loss of the medical images. In most cases, medical images and their integrity are assets of high legal value for the patients as well as hospitals. Therefore, loss of medical fidelity due to DRM practices is highly undesirable.

In this section, we investigate the effects of DRM on sensitive medical information, specifi-cally the effects of digital watermarking on medical image interpretation and disease diagnosis. We describe a computer-aided, automated diagnosis of *malarial infection* from a set of patient blood smear images, and investigate the effects of digital watermarking on those images, in terms of diag-nostic accuracy.

2.1.1 BACKGROUND

In this section we present the necessary background related to (a) digital watermarking and (b) computer-aided automatic diagnosis of malaria.

Digital Watermarking

As mentioned in the previous chapter, watermarking systems are usually *lossy*, that is, a minimum distortion or information-loss of the cover data is unavoidable, with the amount of distortion dependent on the actual algorithm used, the watermark being embedded and the content being watermarked. A primary requirement of general watermarking systems is *imperceptibility*, that is, the distortion of the cover data caused due to watermarking should be minimal and the watermark should be perceptually negligible (Note: a special class of watermarking, known as the *visible or perceptual watermarking* [1], demands that the watermark embedded into the cover data be perceptible). However, in application domains such as the medical industry where data integrity is of utmost importance, the cover data distortion introduced due to watermarking is unacceptable, however minimal or perceptually negligible the distortion is. In such a scenario, lossless or reversible watermarking techniques prove to be useful, which we explore in more detail in this chapter. For example, in 2010 Velumani et al. [31] presented a blind reversible watermarking technique to embed a patient's photograph into a medical image.

Least Significant Bit (LSB) substitution-based watermarking is one of the most primitive and computationally inexpensive methods of general watermarking. In the LSB substitution-based watermark embedding algorithm, the cover image pixels are scanned sequentially, and the LSB of each pixel is substituted by the next watermark bit to be embedded. During extraction, the watermark bits are extracted sequentially from the LSB positions of the cover image pixels. But the original cover image pixel LSBs, once substituted, are permanently lost in the process. Hence, LSB substitution-based watermarking is a lossy watermarking algorithm. We next investigate the impact of digital watermarking, both lossy and reversible, on diagnostic accuracy by an automatic diagnostic model. We would consider LSB substitution to be the representative lossy watermarking algorithm.

Automated Diagnosis of Malaria

In the last few decades, malaria has become a leading cause of death worldwide, having caused 1.5–2.7 million deaths per year [33], most significantly in sub-Saharan Africa and tropical Asia [34]. In today's diagnostic circumstances, pathologists diagnose malarial infection from peripheral blood smear images, under a microscope, based on their clinicopathological knowledge and expertise. This manual procedure is error-prone as well as time-consuming and tedious. To reduce the error probability and time complexity of malaria diagnosis, especially in situations where the disease has taken epidemic proportions, computer-assisted, automated diagnostic systems are being developed, which automatically detect malarial infection from peripheral blood smear images with a high degree of prediction accuracy.

The present state–of–the–art for the existing automatic malaria diagnosis approaches can be traced from the following works. A quantification and classification scheme for *Plasmodium falciparum* infected erythrocytes, is presented by Diaz et al. [35]. Tek et al. proposed a color histogram-based malaria parasite detection [36]. A gray-level thresholding technique for malaria parasite detection was used by Toha et al. [37]. Further, Ross et al. [38] used a morphological thresholding technique for identification of malaria-infected erythrocytes. Makkapati et al. [39] proposed segmentation in the HSV (Hue Saturation Value) color space for the identification of malaria parasite. A mathematical morphology and granulometry-based approach for the estimation of malarial parasitemia was proposed by Dempster et al. [40].

In this chapter, we deal specifically with the diagnosis of malaria caused by the *Plasmodium vivax* parasite. We have used the morphological and textural information based probabilistic model, recently proposed by us in [42]. Our experimental procedure will be presented in Section 2.1.2.

2.1.2 METHODOLOGY

Watermark Embedding and Extraction

In our work, first the original test images were subjected to the automated diagnosis system and then the prediction accuracy was measured. Next, the same images were watermarked using a LSB substitution [43] based general watermarking algorithm. We considered the watermark to be a continuous stream of bits, and substituted the LSBs of the test image pixels by the watermark bits, sequentially. The automatic malarial infection prediction mechanism was then applied to the watermark extracted test images, which contain the residual distortions caused due to the lossy watermarking, and the prediction accuracy was again noted.

In the second phase of our work, the same set of original, undistorted images were reversibly watermarked using the *interpolation-based reversible watermarking* algorithm, proposed in [5]. In this technique, some of the cover image pixels are interpolated based on their neighboring pixels. Such interpolation gives rise to interpolated pixel values as well as interpolation errors. The watermark bits are embedded into the interpolation errors by additive expansion of the errors. The modified errors and interpolated pixels are combined to produce the watermarked pixels. For watermark extraction, the interpolation errors are computed from the watermarked pixels and the watermark bits are extracted from the errors. Those retrieved errors when combined with the interpolated pixel values, restore the original cover image pixels, bit-by-bit. For details of the reversible watermarking technique, the readers are requested to consult the original work by Luo et al. in [5]. Our working methodology is represented in form of a block diagram in Fig. 2.1.

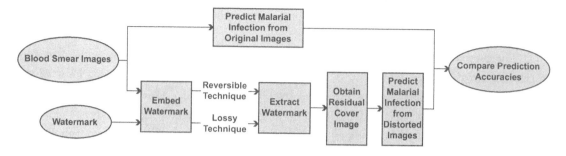

FIGURE 2.1: Work methodology.

Note that since watermark transparency is a primary requirement of any watermarking algorithm, the visual cover–image distortions are usually low. However, due to the image distortions introduced by watermarking, the prediction accuracy can be adversely affected in the case of the images once lossily watermarked, as compared to the original images. Reversible watermarking is expected to provide a solution to this problem. With reversible watermarking, the images can be used in their watermarked form, as well as their original forms, retrieved from the watermarked images. In the above scenario, with the use of reversible watermarking, we can restore the watermarked blood smear images back to their original forms before the prediction. Since this reversal is error-free, that is every bit of the original cover images can be restored to its original form after watermark extraction by reversible watermarking, the prediction accuracy should be as high as what was obtained with the original images. Our experimental results, demonstrating the effects of the aforementioned watermarking algorithms on malarial infection prediction accuracy, are presented in Section 2.1.3. Next, we describe the automated malaria diagnosis system.

Automated Malaria Diagnosis

For our experiment we collected the peripheral blood smear images of 250 patients, from Midnapore Medical College & Hospital and Medipath Laboratory, West Bengal, India. According to the physicians' suggestions, of those 250 blood smear images we used 50 as our test images, which were the least noisy and whose slides were the best prepared. Median filtering [44] was applied on our 50 test images, specifically on their green (G) component, to their reduce impulse noise further. Since the green (G) channel of a color image provides more information than its red (R) or blue (B) channels, we used the green component of the test images in our experiment.

Erythrocytes, being the area of interest for detection of *Plasmodium vivax* infection in blood, were segmented from the blood smear images, using a gray-level thresholding method proposed by Otsu [45]. Next, the unwanted cells like leukocyte and platelets were eliminated from the blood

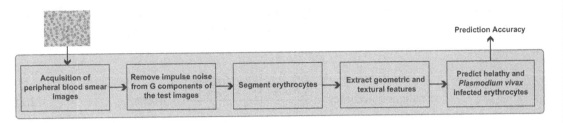

FIGURE 2.2: Experimental procedure.

smear images by morphological operators. Finally the overlapping erythrocytes were segmented by the *marker controlled watershed algorithm* [46].

After the segmentation was complete we extracted some features from the processed test images to identify the infected and non-infected erythrocytes. We selected a total of 26 different features, significant enough to discriminate the classes. Those features include geometrical features such as area, parameter, compactness, circularity, etc., as well as *Haralick textural features* [47] such as *difference entropy*, *contrast*, *correlation*, *dissimilarity*, etc. The erythrocytes were inferred to be healthy or *Plasmodium vivax* infected from these set of 26 geometrical and textural features, by the use of *multivariate logistic regression* model [48]. The entire experimental procedure is shown in Fig. 2.2, with the help of a block diagram.

We have carried out the experiment on three different data sets, as described in Section 2.1.2:

- the set of 50 original blood smear images;

- the images obtained by watermarking those 50 blood smear images by LSB substitution [43], and subsequently extracting the watermark from those images; and

- on the images reversibly watermarked by Luo et al.'s [5] interpolation-based algorithm, and subsequently restored to their original forms after watermark extraction.

The total number of healthy and infected erythrocytes were constant for all three test image sets. Our test data consisted of total 90 infected and 186 healthy erythrocytes, for each of the 3 sets.

For each of the three above cases, we measured the prediction accuracy and compared them. The prediction accuracy of the healthy erythrocytes is measured as $\frac{P_{healthy}}{N_{heathy}} \times 100\%$, where $P_{healthy}$ is the number of erythrocytes predicted as healthy by our experiment, and N_{heathy} is the actual number of healthy erythrocytes. Similarly, the prediction accuracy of the infected erythrocytes is measured as $\frac{P_{infected}}{N_{infected}} \times 100\%$, where $P_{infected}$ is the number of erythrocytes predicted as infected by our experiment, and $N_{infected}$ is the actual number of healthy erythrocytes. Note here that the parameters $P_{healthy}$ and $P_{infected}$ are not defined globally over the entire set of erythrocytes. Rather,

$P_{healthy}$ and $P_{infected}$ are parameters defined (to predict diagnostic accuracy) exclusively for the sets of healthy and infected erythrocytes, respectively. The overall prediction accuracy is computed as the average:

$$\text{Prediction accuracy} = \frac{\left(\frac{P_{healthy}}{N_{heathy}}\right) + \left(\frac{P_{infected}}{N_{infected}}\right)}{2} \times 100\%. \qquad (2.1)$$

For our test data sets, $N_{heathy} = 186$ and $N_{infected} = 90$.

2.1.3   RESULTS

Figure 2.3 shows an original blood smear image, and the image watermarked by LSB substitution-based lossy watermarking. The size of watermark embedded by LSB substitution and the cover image distortion, averaged across all 50 test images, are presented in Table 2.1. In our experiment, the erythrocytes are segmented from the G component of the blood smear images. Hence, the distortion and the amount of information embedded into the G component of the test images play an important role in our experimental results. These data have also been specified in Table 2.1. All data presented in Table 2.1 are the averages over all 50 test images. We have measured the watermark size in terms of bits-per-pixel (bpp) and the image distortion in terms of Peak-Signal-to-Noise-Ratio (PSNR).

In Figs. 2.4–2.7 we present the *class-condition density plots* [48] of the healthy and *Plasmodium vivax* infected erythrocytes, corresponding to four arbitrarily selected features. The class-condition density plots represent the likelihood area of the healthy and infected erythrocytes in form of their probability density functions. The four features selected by us are *entropy, homogeneity, difference entropy,* and *inverse difference normalized*, which are represented by dimensionless numeric values, as shown on the X-axes of the plots in Figs. 2.4–2.7. For detailed procedure of calculation of those Haralick textural features, the readers are requested to consult the referred work in [47]. Y-axes of the plots in Figs. 2.4–2.7 represent the probability density values of the four features, estimated by

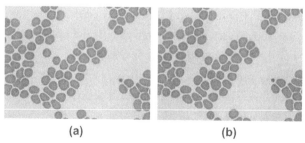

(a)   (b)

FIGURE 2.3: (a) Original blood smear image; (b) blood smear image watermarked by LSB substitution.

TABLE 2.1: Watermarked image distortions, residual distortions (after watermark extraction), and embedded watermark size[a]

Algorithm	Watermarked Image Distortion (PSNR)		Residual Distortion (PSNR)		Embedded bpp	
	Entire Image	G Component	Entire Image	G Component	Entire Image	G Component
Luo et al.'s [5] interpolation-based reversible watermarking	49.84 dB	54.10 dB	Zero distortion	Zero distortion	2.17	0.78

a. All data averaged over 50 test images.

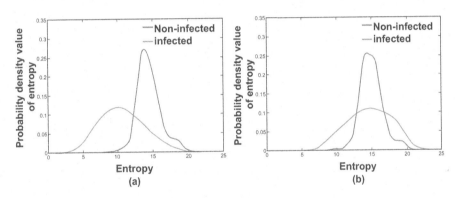

FIGURE 2.4: Class-condition density plots of feature *entropy*, for (a) original and (b) distorted test images.

Kernel Density Estimation [49]. For each feature, the class-condition density plots for the original test images and test images containing residual distortions after lossy watermark extraction are presented in subfigures (a) and (b), respectively. From the class-condition density plot of a particular feature, the overlap between the likelihood areas of the infected and non-infected classes of erythrocytes are observed. The larger the area of overlap, the lower the overall prediction accuracy. It can be observed that for all four features shown in Figs. 2.4–2.7, the area of overlap is higher for the distorted images, compared to the original images. Hence, when all 26 features are combined to predict the healthy and infected erythrocytes in our experiment, the prediction accuracy is considerably higher for the original images, as compared to the images containing some residual distortions, caused by lossy watermarking, remaining even after the watermark was extracted.

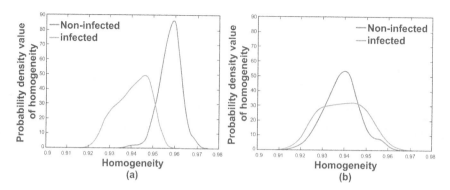

FIGURE 2.5: Class-condition density plots of feature *homogeneity* for (a) original and (b) distorted test images.

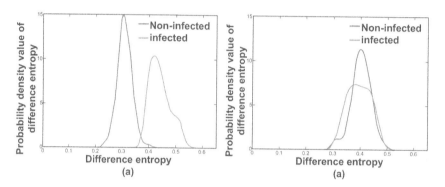

FIGURE 2.6: Class-condition density plots of feature *difference entropy* for (a) original and (b) distorted test images.

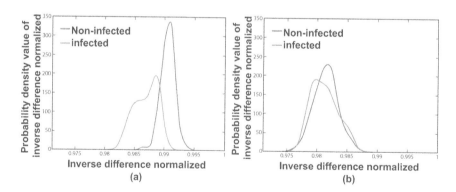

FIGURE 2.7: Class-condition density plots of feature *inverse difference normalized* for (a) original and (b) distorted test images.

TABLE 2.2: Prediction statistics of healthy and *Plasmodium vivax* infected erythrocytes, for original test images

| | | Actual | | |
		Infected	Healthy	Prediction Accuracy (%)
Predicted	Infected	79	11	87.78
	Healthy	8	178	95.70
	Overall Prediction Accuracy (%)			91.74

TABLE 2.3: Prediction statistics of healthy and *Plasmodium vivax* infected erythrocytes, for test images containing residual distortion, caused due to lossy watermarking and subsequent watermark extraction

| | | Actual | | |
		Infected	Healthy	Prediction Accuracy (%)
Predicted	Infected	74	16	82.22
	Healthy	12	174	93.54
	Overall Prediction Accuracy (%)			87.88

The accuracy of predicting the healthy and infected erythrocytes, for the original and distorted sets of test images are reported in Tables 2.2 and 2.3, respectively. Tables 2.2 and 2.3 show that the overall prediction accuracy for the original test images is 91.74%, whereas the overall prediction accuracy for the distorted test images is 87.88%. Thus, our experimental results prove that the prediction accuracy is considerably lower for the distorted blood smear images, as compared to the original images. In order to avoid erroneous diagnosis of diseases, the prediction accuracy of such clinical tests need to be high enough. Hence, from these experimental results we conclude that LSB replacement-based and similar lossy watermarking schemes might not be the best choice for medical records for which accuracy is a crucial issue.

To demonstrate the effect of reversible watermarking, we watermarked the same set of 50 blood smear images using Luo et al.'s [5] *interpolation*-based reversible watermarking algorithm. Next, the watermark was extracted from the reversibly watermarked images and they were restored to their original forms by Luo et al.'s [5] reversible watermark extraction algorithm. (Note here

TABLE 2.4: Prediction statistics of healthy and *Plasmodium vivax* infected erythrocytes, for test images, reversibly watermarked and subsequently restored to their original forms after watermark extraction

		Actual		
		Infected	Healthy	Prediction Accuracy (%)
Predicted	Infected	79	11	87.78
	Healthy	8	178	95.70
	Overall Prediction Accuracy (%)			91.74

that the images restored by reversible watermarking after watermark extraction contain zero residual distortions, according to inherent property of reversible watermarking.) Our experimental procedure described in Section 2.1.2 was applied to those restored test images. The restored test images contained zero residual distortion, according to the inherent property of reversible watermarking; and, as expected, the prediction accuracy achieved was the same as that obtained in case of the original, non-watermarked images. The prediction accuracy achieved with the test images restored by reversible watermarking is presented in Table 2.4. Hence, we conclude that reversible watermarking, in spite of being generally computationally more involved than lossy watermarking schemes (as would be evident from later chapters) is a better choice for medical imaging where accuracy is crucial.

2.1.4   INFERENCES: EFFECT OF LOSSY WATERMARKING SCHEME ON AUTOMATED MALARIA DIAGNOSIS

It was observed from our experimental results that the information-loss caused by a lossy watermarking scheme results in reduced accuracy of an automated diagnosis scheme for malaria. Specifically, we demonstrated the adverse effect of information-loss caused by a simple lossy watermarking scheme on the prediction accuracy of malarial infection, vis-a-vis the effect of a lossless reversible watermarking scheme. Such information-loss, residual even after watermark extraction, is undesirable in the medical industry, since it deals with highly sensitive data. Our experimental results prove that the accuracy of malaria diagnosis from the blood smear images, restored by reversible watermarking, is as high as what is achieved in case of the original images. Thus, it is inferred that reversible watermarking algorithms are preferable over general watermarking algorithms in medical applications dealing with sensitive imagery.

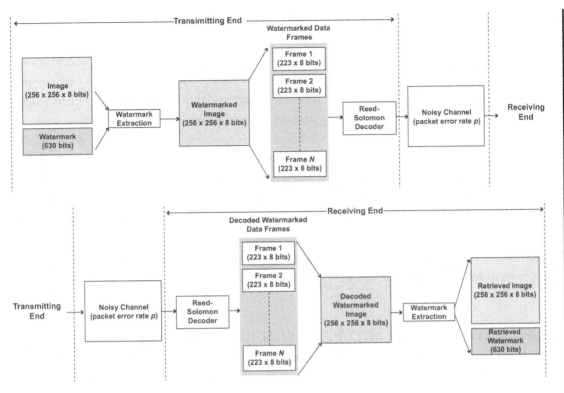

FIGURE 2.8: Experiment setup.

2.2 INVESTIGATING PERFORMANCE IN NOISY MILITARY ENVIRONMENT

Reversible digital watermarking techniques enable the recovery of the original "cover image" from a watermarked image in a distortion-free way. Reversible watermarking techniques find application in military and medical imagery, where integrity of the cover image is of utmost importance. However, in many cases, in spite of using a reversible watermarking technique, bit-by-bit recovery of the cover image may be infeasible. For example, military communication often takes place over highly noisy channels (e.g., over a temporary, low-bandwidth radio data-link setup in the battlefield or near enemy territory). Research indicates that packet error rates of such channels can be as high as 30% [61, 62, 63, 64]. In such scenarios, it might not be possible to correct all errors at the receiver end, in spite of using error-correcting codes. Consequently, we are bound to get non-zero distortion in the recovered cover image as well as the extracted watermark, in spite of using reversible watermarking techniques.

In the rest of this chapter, we investigate the effect of high data error rates on images watermarked using different state-of-the-art reversible watermarking algorithms [68], vis-a-vis non-watermarked images. We would find that digital images processed by most reversible watermarking schemes have greater residual noise robustness than non-watermarked images. In the next section, we investigate (through simulations) the distortion characteristics of reversibly watermarked images which are transmitted over highly noisy channels. We consider several watermarking schemes which have been recently published and investigate their performances in this particular scenario. Usually, (a) data embedding capacity, (b) ease of watermark embedding (and extraction), and (c) the amount of distortion due to watermark embedding are the performance factors which are considered while evaluating any watermarking scheme. Given the particular application domain (military communication) of reversible watermarking, we feel that this study is important to evaluate the relative acceptability of schemes in such extreme environments, and more importantly, the acceptability of reversible watermarking itself in adverse situations which might arise in its particular application domain (military imaging).

2.2.1   EXPERIMENTAL SETUP AND SIMULATION RESULTS

Here we present our experimental setup and simulation results to investigate the distortion characteristics of the original image and watermark when transmitted through a noisy channel with high *packet error rate* (PER) p. Here, p refers to the percentage of pixels, distorted in each frame. Our experimental setup is shown in Fig. 2.8. One representative watermarking scheme, for each of the algorithms described in the last section, was implemented in MATLAB. A noisy communication channel with a given PER was simulated in MATLAB by inducing random bit-flipping of the pixels within the data packets such that the percentage of pixels distorted in each data packet, transmitted over the channel, is equal to the given PER. The simulations were carried out on six 256×256 grayscale standard test images, as shown in Fig. 2.9. A random bitstream of size 630 bits was selected as the watermark. The maximum watermark embedding capacity varies with each scheme as well as with each cover image. To make the comparisons fair, we have selected a uniform watermark for all watermarking algorithms and for all images. The size of the watermark was selected to be 630 bits, since this length is the maximum that could be embedded into each image using any of the algorithms analyzed. Note here that, among all the watermarking schemes, Ni et al.'s [20] histogram bin-shifting technique provides the minimum embedding capacity, for all our test images. Among our test images *Mandrill*, having the minimum correlation among its pixels, has minimum watermark embedding capacity for all watermarking schemes. A watermark of length 630 bits was the maximum that could be embedded into the 256×256 *Mandrill* image using the histogram bin shifting technique.

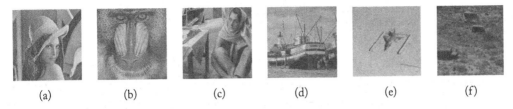

FIGURE 2.9: The test images: (a) *Lena*; (b) *Mandrill*; (c) *Barbara*; (d) *Barche*; (e) *Jet*; and (f) *Field*. ((a) Model courtesy of *Playboy Magazine*, 1972; (b)–(f) Computer Vision Group, University of Granada)

In our experiment, the representative scheme from each class of reversible watermarking algorithm was used to embed a watermark of size 630 bits into each of our test images. The watermarked image was then transmitted through the simulated noisy channel. Following are the input and output parameters for each representative watermarking algorithm in our experiment.

Input Parameters:

Cover Image $I \in \{$ *Lena, Mandrill, Barbara, Barche, Jet, Field* $\}$;

Watermark W s.t. $|W| = 630$;

PER p of the simulated noisy transmission channel, s.t. p varies over $[0, 0.25]$.

Output Parameter:

Retrieved Image I_R; Extracted Watermark W_R.

Experimental Steps:

1. The watermarked image, produced by embedding W into I, was broken down into data frames containing 223 (grayscale) pixels.

2. Each frame was appended with 32 redundant unsigned 8-bit integers, for error detection and correction at the receiver side. We employed the widely used (255,223)-*Reed–Solomon encoding* scheme [65] for error detection and correction.

3. Each encoded frame was transmitted through the simulated noisy channel. We have varied the PER of the channel, from 0–25%.

4. At the receiver side, each frame was decoded using Reed–Solomon decoder to retrieve a 223–grayscale pixel frame and then the watermarked image was restored by combining those received frames.

5. Finally, the original cover image I_R was retrieved and the watermark W_R extracted from the watermarked image.

We estimated the distortion of the cover image by computing the *Mean Square Error* (MSE) of the pixel values as

$$\text{MSE} = \frac{\sum_{i=1}^{m} \sum_{j=1}^{n} \left(X_{org}(i, j) - X_{wm}(i, j)\right)^2}{m \cdot n}, \tag{2.2}$$

where $X_{org}(i, j)$ is the (i, j)–th pixel of the original image, and $X_{wm}(i, j)$ is the (i, j)–th pixel of the watermarked image, and m and n are the dimensions of the image (here each is 256). The distortion in the watermark was estimated by the percentage of bits altered after extraction. The reason for using a different, non pixel-value-based metric for the watermark is that the watermark is a bitstream that helps to authenticate the original image. If the watermark to be embedded is another image, its pixel values are converted into their binary representations, which are then concatenated to form a bitstream to form the watermark. Figures 2.10 and 2.11 show the distortion vs. channel error probability plots, for the cover image and watermark, respectively. To avoid any bias that could arise from a single experiment, we have performed 100 simulations for each value of channel error probability. The cover image distortion (MSE) and watermark distortion (% of bits flipped) for each value of channel error probability (PER $p \in [0, 0.25]$), shown in Figs. 2.10 and 2.11, respectively, are the average of all 100 simulations.

To present the variations in cover image distortion and watermark distortion over 100 simulations, we have produced interval plots for cover image MSE and % of watermark bits flipped, for one of our test images, the 256×256 *Lena* image. The interval plots of cover image distortion (MSE) and watermark distortion (% of bits flipped), are presented in Figs. 2.12 and 2.13, respectively. The interval plot for each watermarking algorithm is shown in a separate subfigure for clarity. The intervals shown in Figs. 2.12 and 2.13 with vertical line segments represent the distortion variations over the 100 simulations, whereas the dots represent the average distortions for each value of channel error probability.

2.2.2   DISCUSSION

1. Up to the PER of approximately 7%, the MSE of the cover images as well as percentage distortion of the watermark bits remain fixed at zero. This is in compliance with the theoretical error correcting capability of $(255, 223)$–Reed–Solomon codes. The error correcting capability of (n, k)–Reed–Solomon encoding being up to $\frac{(n-k)}{2}$ frame elements [65], in our simulation environment up to $\frac{(255-223)}{2} = 16 \approx (0.07 \times 223)$ distorted pixels can be corrected in each frame.

2. At higher PERs, the number of pixels distorted by the simulated noisy channel increases linearly. Thus, the MSE of the cover image increases *almost* linearly with error probability (for all watermarking schemes). Note that the increase in MSE of the cover image is not *exactly* linear. This is due to two reasons. First, the randomness in selection of pixel positions to be distorted in each frame. Second, the randomness in selection of number and position of bit(s)

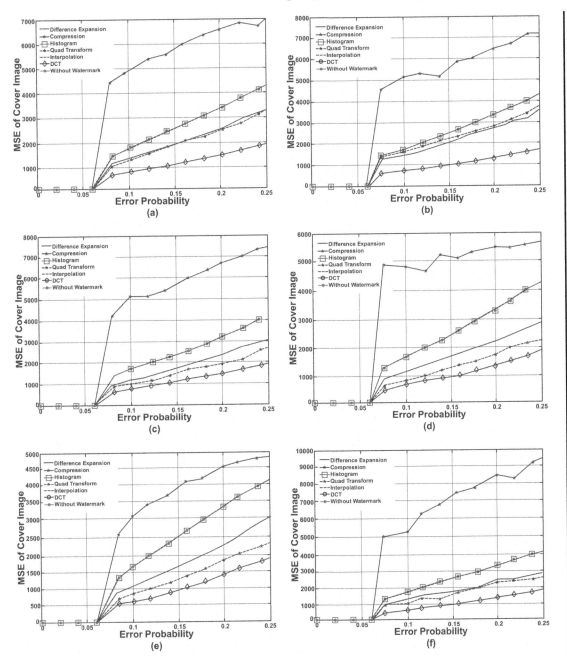

FIGURE 2.10: Variation of MSE of test cover images: (a) *Lena*; (b) *Mandrill*; (c) *Barbara*; (d) *Barche*; (e) *Jet*; and (f) *Field* with increase in packet error rate of the transmission channel.

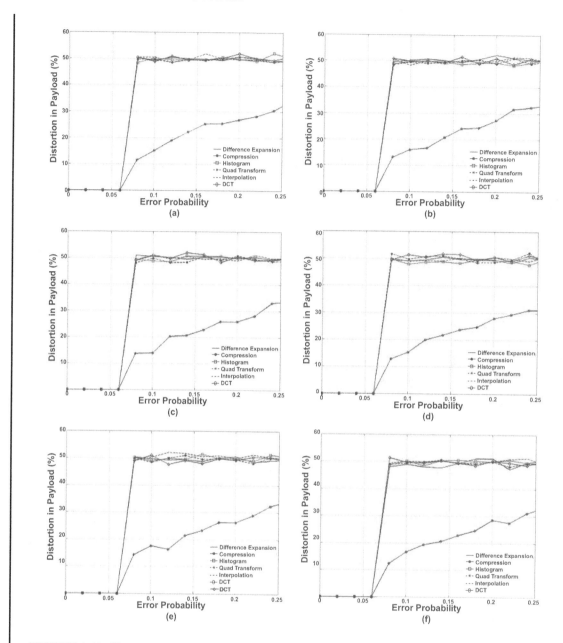

FIGURE 2.11: Variation in percentage of bits flipped in watermark, extracted from the watermarked test cover images: (a) *Lena*; (b) *Mandrill*; (c) *Barbara*; (d) *Barche*; (e) *Jet*; and (f) *Field* with increase in packet error rate of the transmission channel.

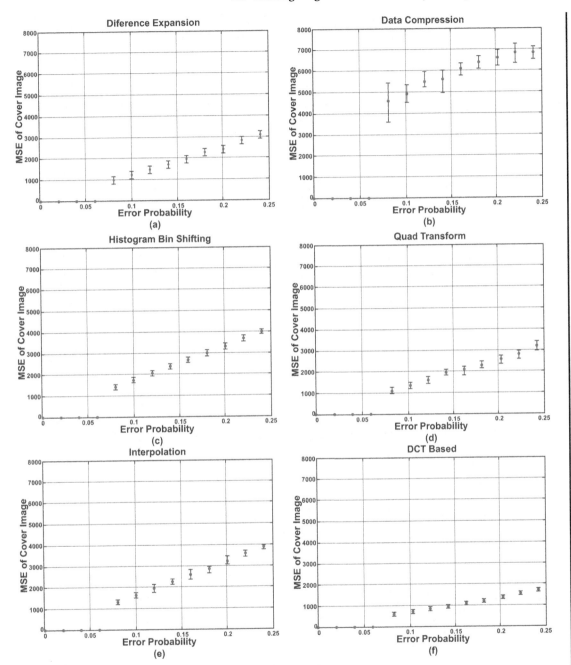

FIGURE 2.12: **Interval plots** for variation of MSE of *Lena* image, watermarked using: (a) *Difference Expansion*; (b) *Data Compression*; (c) *Histogram Bin Shifting*; (d) *Quad Transform*; (e) *Interpolation* and (f) *DCT-Based Watermarking*.

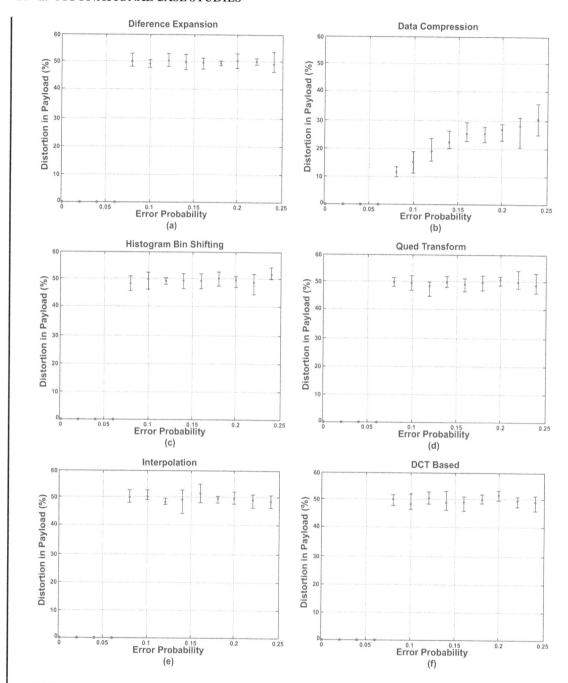

FIGURE 2.13: **Interval plots** for variation in percentage of bits flipped in the watermark extracted from the *Lena* image using: (a) *Difference Expansion*; (b) *Data Compression*; (c) *Histogram Bin Shifting*; (d) *Quad Transform*; (e) *Interpolation* and (f) *DCT-Based Watermarking*.

to be distorted in each pixel. This randomness is introduced in our experimental procedure, in order to simulate a real life noisy channel [61, 62, 63, 64, 66], where the position(s) of error(s) inserted in each data packet is random. In our implementation randomness is generated by MATLAB built-in function RANDERR.

3. The rate of increase of MSE for algorithms using data compression is the highest (higher than the rate of increase of MSE for images without any watermark). The algorithms using data compression [14, 16] that we have analyzed compress a number of (lowermost) bit planes to make space for embedding the watermark. The compressed bit planes are embedded into the empty space as a part of the watermark. The number of bit planes compressed is generally more than one, in order to provide large embedding capacity (even by single layer embedding) as compared to other classes of spatial domain reversible watermarking algorithms. For example, in our implementation, we compressed three lowermost bit planes of the cover image. Thus, when the watermark extracted is erroneous due to the noise in the transmission channel, a large part of the original cover image, which was embedded as a part of the watermark, also gets distorted giving rise to such a high rate of increase of cover image MSE.

4. Images watermarked with the classes of algorithms based on histogram bin shifting as well as pixel value interpolation exhibit approximately the same performance as that of the non-watermarked images. In algorithms based on histogram bin shifting technique, only a fraction of the total number of pixels are modified by just adding one to their values. So the watermarked image is very close to the original image in terms of pixel values. This justifies the fact that the behavior of the images, watermarked with this class of reversible watermarking algorithms is similar to that of the non-watermarked images.

   A similar case is for interpolation-based reversible watermarking algorithms [5] where the number of pixels altered for watermark embedding is equal to the size of the watermark in bits. The additive increase of interpolation errors causes only a fraction of the total number of pixels to have their values increased by one and the rest remain unaltered. Thus, for both these schemes such small distortions due to watermarking becomes negligible in comparison to the large distortions caused by the noisy transmission channel.

5. The rate of increase of MSE for algorithms using DCT and integer transform (difference expansion and quad transform) perform well, with their rate of increase of MSE being lower than that for non-watermarked images. Among these, algorithms using DCT has the lowest rate of increase of MSE. In integer transform-based reversible watermarking algorithms, each watermark bit is embedded by expanding the differences between two (for Tian's difference expansion [4, 10]) or four (for Weng et al.'s quad transform [11]) neighboring pixels. The process of difference expansion by the sender and subsequent difference restoration by the

receiver to recover the original cover image causes some of its distorted pixels to get recovered, which could never be recovered from the same image watermarked by some other scheme without the difference expansion–restoration property. The difference expansion–restoration procedure being an inherent property of the integer transform-based reversible watermarking algorithms, even a non-watermarked image exhibits higher distortion compared to images reversibly watermarked by integer transform.

We observe that the DCT-based reversible watermarking algorithm allows the most faithful recovery of the original cover image. This can be inferred to be due to the superior energy compaction and decorrelation properties of the two-dimensional DCT [67], which has been used in this algorithm [6]. In our experimental results, the DCT-based reversible watermarking algorithm exhibits the minimum residual distortion of the cover image, which is much lower compared to the distortions produced by all the other spatial domain algorithms.

6. The percentage of distorted watermark bits remains almost constant at 50% and its rate of change is almost equal for all classes of algorithms, except data compression, which gives remarkably lower watermark distortion at lower error rates, although the distortion increases linearly with increasing error rate. In data compression-based reversible watermarking algorithms, the watermark bits are first converted into L-ary symbols and then embedded into the cover image. In all other classes of reversible watermarking algorithms, the watermark is embedded as a raw, unprocessed bitstream. Hence, the percentage of distorted watermark bits for the data compression-based algorithm increases linearly with the increase in channel error probability.

2.2.3   SUMMARY

In the second half of this chapter, we presented a (simulation-based) distortion characteristics comparison of reversibly watermarked images, when subjected to transmission over highly noisy channels. Our simulation results show that in such an environment, DCT-based schemes allow cover image retrieval with the least distortion, whereas to retrieve the watermark with minimum distortion, schemes based on data compression are the most suitable. Interestingly, most reversible watermarking schemes show less residual error than non-watermarked images. This implies that reversible watermarking does not adversely affect the image fidelity when transmitted over a highly noisy channel.

CHAPTER 3

Overview of State-of-the-Art Reversible Watermarking Techniques

3.1 INTRODUCTION

This chapter presents an overview of the state-of-the-art digital reversible watermarking technology. The overwhelming majority of the reversible watermarking algorithms until now have been developed for grayscale digital images, and we will describe the same. In 2006, Feng et al. [8] classified reversible watermarking algorithms into three broad classes, depending on their principles of operation, viz. *Reversible Watermarking by Data Compression*, *Reversible Watermarking by Difference Expansion*, and *Reversible Watermarking by Histogram-Bin-Shifting*.

In this chapter we modify Feng et al. [8]'s three-way classification, taking into account the more recently developed *spatial domain* techniques as well as *frequency domain* techniques. Here we present the following five major techniques of reversible watermarking, with outline of the corresponding watermark embedding and extraction procedures:

1. *Difference Expansion*

2. *Data Compression*

3. *Histogram-Bin-Shifting*

4. *Pixel Prediction*

5. *Modification of Frequency Domain Characteristic*

However, the above list does not imply strict or mutually exclusive division of reversible watermarking algorithms into those categories. More than one of the above techniques may be utilized for operation of a particular reversible watermarking scheme. In other words, a scheme may fall into one or more of the above categories.

The rest of the chapter is organized as follows. We present the operating principles of the above five categories of reversible watermarking algorithms (representing each class by an example) in Sections 3.2–3.6. The chapter will be concluded in Section 5.5.

3.2   DIFFERENCE EXPANSION

This class of reversible watermarking algorithms [4, 10, 11, 12] takes advantage of the usually large spatial redundancy in the grayscale values of neighboring pixels in an image. Here, we take the example of Tian's [4, 10] reversible watermarking by *Difference Expansion*, which is based on *Integer Haar Transform*. In Tian's difference expansion algorithm the average (l) and difference (h) of two adjacent pixel values x and y are computed as $l = \left\lfloor \frac{x+y}{2} \right\rfloor$ and $h = x - y$, respectively. The reverse integer transforms to get back the exact pixel values, x and y, from l and h are: $x = l + \left\lfloor \frac{h+1}{2} \right\rfloor$ and $y = l - \left\lfloor \frac{h}{2} \right\rfloor$. Here, the difference between two adjacent pixels is *expanded* by multiplication by 2. This expansion creates space (in the LSB of the expanded difference) for a watermark bit to be embedded.

Embedding Algorithm

The reversible watermark embedding algorithm by difference expansion is presented in Procedure 1 (**DIFF_EXP_EMBED**). The reversible watermark embedding algorithm by difference expansion starts by computing average (l) and difference (h) for each consecutive pixel pair. Here the *difference numbers* are categorized into three classes.

Expandable. Those difference numbers, whose binary representations when left shifted by 1 bit and a payload bit (0 or 1) is embedded in the LSB (least significant bit) position, preserve the property that the pixel values computed from it are in the range $[0, 2^b - 1]$ (where bit-depth of the cover image is b). The *left shift and embed* operation is called *expansion*.

Changeable. Those difference numbers which preserve the property that the pixel values computed from it are in the range $[0, 2^b - 1]$, irrespective of the payload bit (0 or 1) used to replace its Least Significant Bit (LSB). Note here that *expandability* implies *changeability*, but the reverse is not always true.

Not Changeable. Difference numbers which are not changeable, hence also not expandable.

A *location map*, a data structure keeping track of the expandable pixels, is created and is initially empty. For each difference number (h), a 1 is appended to the *location map* if the difference number is expandable, otherwise a 0 is appended to it. The location map is losslessly compressed to create bitstream L. *Run Length Encoding (RLE)* and *JBIG2* [13] are the suggested compression methods. The LSBs of all changeable h's are concatenated to form the bitstream C. Further, L, C and the watermark bits are concatenated to form the bitstream B.

Now, for each h, if it is expandable, it is expanded to embed the next bit of B; otherwise, if it is changeable, its LSB is replaced with the next bit of B. Difference numbers which are not

Procedure 1: DIFF_EXP_EMBED

Input: Original cover image $\mathcal{I}$ of size $m \times n$ pixels represented by b bits each; Watermark $\mathcal{W}$;

Output: Watermarked image

```
// Create location map and collect LSBs of changeable difference numbers;
```

1   Initialize all elements of array $loc\_map[0 .. m \times n]$ to zero;

2   Initialize empty array C to collect LSBs of changeable difference numbers;

3   **foreach** consecutive pixel pair (x, y) of $\mathcal{I}$ **do**

4   Compute average $l = \left\lfloor \frac{x+y}{2} \right\rfloor$; difference $h = x - y$;

5   **if** $|2h + w| \le min(2(2^b - 1 - l), 2l + 1) \; \forall w \in [0, 1]$ **then**   `// h is expandable`

6   Set next element of loc_map to 1;

7   **else if** $|2 \left\lfloor \frac{h}{2} \right\rfloor + w| \le min(2(2^b - 1 - l), 2l + 1) \; \forall w \in [0, 1]$ **then**   `// h is changeable`

                                                                                 `// but not expandable`

8   Set next element of C to LSB(h);

```
// Create payload
```

9   Losslessly compress loc_map to L;

10   Create payload $B = \text{Concatenate}(L, C, W)$;

```
// Embed payload
```

11   **foreach** consecutive pixel pair (x, y) of $\mathcal{I}$ **do**

12   Compute average $l = \left\lfloor \frac{x+y}{2} \right\rfloor$; difference $h = x - y$;

13   **if** $|2h + w| \le min(2(2^b - 1 - l), 2l + 1) \; \forall w \in [0, 1]$ **then**   `// h is expandable`

14         $h = 2h + (\text{next element of } \mathcal{W})$;   `// Left shift and embed next watermark bit`

15   **else if** $|2 \left\lfloor \frac{h}{2} \right\rfloor + w| \le min(2(2^b - 1 - l), 2l + 1) \; \forall w \in [0, 1]$ **then**   `// h is changeable`

                                                                                 `// but not expandable`

16         $h = 2 \left\lfloor \frac{h}{2} \right\rfloor + (\text{next element of } \mathcal{W})$;   `// Embed next watermark bit by LSB replacement`

17   Obtain watermarked pixel pair (x, y) by reverse transform: $x = l + \left\lfloor \frac{h+1}{2} \right\rfloor$; $y = l - \left\lfloor \frac{h}{2} \right\rfloor$;

changeable, hence neither expandable, are not used for embedding; they remain unmodified after cover image watermarking.

Extraction Algorithm

The difference expansion based watermark extraction process is presented in Procedure 2 (**DIFF_EXP_EXTRACT**). During watermark extraction, similar to the embedding process, the difference and average of each consecutive pixel pair is computed. Now, the LSBs of the changeable difference numbers are collected into the bitstream B. This B is nothing but the concatenation of three different bitstreams: (1) the compressed location map (L); (2) LSBs of originally changeable but

Procedure 2: DIFF_EXP_EXTRACT

Input: Watermarked image $\mathcal{I}_W$ of size $m \times n$ pixels represented by b bits each;
Output: Retrieved cover image; Extracted watermark;

// Extract payload
1 Initialize empty array B to collect payload bits;
2 **foreach** consecutive pixel pair (x, y) of $\mathcal{I}_W$ **do**
3   Compute average $l = \left\lfloor \frac{x+y}{2} \right\rfloor$; difference $h = x - y$;
4   **if** $|2 \left\lfloor \frac{h}{2} \right\rfloor + w| \leq min(2(2^b - 1 - l), 2l + 1) \; \forall w \in [0, 1]$ **then**   // h is changeable
5   Set next element of $B = mod(h, 2)$;   // Collect LSBs of all changeable difference numbers

// Extract watermark
6 From B, extract L (compressed location map), C (LSBs of original changeable but not expandable difference numbers before watermarking) and the watermark;

// Restore cover image
7 Decompress L to loc_map;
8 Initialize $pointer = 0$;
9 **foreach** consecutive pixel pair (x, y) of $\mathcal{I}_W$ **do**
10   Compute average $l = \left\lfloor \frac{x+y}{2} \right\rfloor$; difference $h = x - y$;
11     $pointer = pointer + 1$;   // Point to the next element of loc_map
12   **if** Set next element of $loc\_map = 1$ **then**   // h was expandable before watermarking
13   Restore $h = \left\lfloor \frac{h}{2} \right\rfloor$;   // Right shift
14   **else if** $loc\_map(pointer) = 0$ and $|2 \left\lfloor \frac{h}{2} \right\rfloor + b| \leq min(2(2^b - 1 - l), 2l + 1) \; \forall b \in [0, 1]$ **then**
           // h was changeable but not expandable before watermarking
15   Restore $h = 2 \left\lfloor \frac{h}{2} \right\rfloor + $ (next element of C);   // Restore original LSB
16   Restore original pixel pair (x, y) by reverse transform: $x = l + \left\lfloor \frac{h+1}{2} \right\rfloor$; $y = l - \left\lfloor \frac{h}{2} \right\rfloor$;

---

not expandable difference numbers (C); and (3) the watermark ($\mathcal{W}$). The watermark, along with L and C, are extracted from B.

To restore the cover image pixels, we restore the original difference numbers and apply reverse integer transform on the average-difference pairs. The expandable difference numbers are restored by right-shifting, and the changeable difference numbers are restored by restoring their original LSBs. The expandable and changeable difference numbers are differentiated by the location map, obtained by decompressing L.

3.3 DATA COMPRESSION

Algorithms proposed in [14, 15, 16, 17, 18] belong to this class of reversible watermarking algorithms, which compress some of the *bit planes* of the cover image matrix to make space for watermark embedding. The bit planes altered are the lowest ones, so that the distortion caused in the cover image is perceptually negligible. In this class of reversible watermarking algorithms, for embedding into L lowest bit planes of the cover image matrix, an L-level quantization is applied to the cover image pixels and the watermark bitstream is converted to a sequence of L-ary symbols. We consider Celik et al.'s [14] data compression based reversible watermarking technique to represent this class.

Embedding Algorithm

The data compression-based reversible watermark embedding algorithm is presented in Procedure 3 (**DATA_COMPRESSION_EMBED**). The algorithm applies an L-level quantization on the cover image $\mathcal{I}$, to obtain a quantized matrix $Q_L(\mathcal{I})$ and a sequence of quantization remainders $r_L(\mathcal{I})$ (steps 1–4). The remainders $r_L(\mathcal{I})$ are losslessly compressed (for example, by *LZW* encoding [19]) into a shorter bitstream $r_L^C(\mathcal{I})$, which is then appended with the watermark bits to generate the bitstream H (steps 5–7). Next, H is converted to a sequence of L-ary symbols $\in \{0, 1, \cdots, L-1\}$, which are finally added to the quantized pixel values constituting $Q_L(\mathcal{I})$, to produce the watermarked image matrix $\mathcal{I}'$ (steps 8–15).

To convert H into L-ary symbols, we first initialize an interval $R = [0,1)$ in step 8. Next, for each pixel $\mathcal{I}(i, j)$ of the cover image $\mathcal{I}$, we compute the maximum number of levels N_L, available for embedding watermark bits into $\mathcal{I}(i, j)$ (step 11). R is divided into N_L equal sub intervals, from which the sub interval R_S is chosen, such that $H \in R_S$ (steps 12–13). $S \in [0, N_L - 1]$ represents nothing but the next L-ary payload symbol, which is embedded into the next cover image pixel, in step 14. After each iteration, corresponding to one pixel of $\mathcal{I}$, interval R is reset to the last value of R_S (step 15).

Extraction Algorithm

The data compression based reversible watermark extraction algorithm is presented in Procedure 4 (**DATA_COMPRESSION_EXTRACT**). In the extraction algorithm, the watermarked image $\mathcal{I}'$ is L-level quantized to produce the quantized matrix $Q_L(\mathcal{I}')$ and a sequence quantization remainders $r_L(\mathcal{I}')$ (steps 1–4). Next, the bitstream H, which was originally produced by concatenation of watermark bits to the compressed original quantization remainders, is recovered in steps 5–12.

To recover bitstream H, in Procedure 4, interval R is initialized to $[0,1)$ in step 5. Next, for each pixel $\mathcal{I}'(i, j)$ of the watermarked image $\mathcal{I}'$, we compute the maximum number of levels N_L, available for embedding watermark bits into $\mathcal{I}'(i, j)$ (step 8). R is divided into N_L equal sub intervals

---

Procedure 3: DATA_COMPRESSION_EMBED

Input: Original cover image $\mathcal{I}$ of size $m \times n$ pixels represented by b bits each;
             Watermark $\mathcal{W}$ in form of binary bitstream;
Output: Watermarked image $\mathcal{I}'$;

    // Quantize cover image
1 **for** $i = 1$ **to** m **do**
2   **for** $j = 1$ **to** n **do**
3        $Q_L(\mathcal{I}(i,j)) = L \left\lfloor \frac{\mathcal{I}(i,j)}{L} \right\rfloor$;   // $\mathcal{I}(i,j)$ represents the (i,j)-th pixel of $\mathcal{I}$
4        $r_L(\mathcal{I}(i,j)) = \mathcal{I}(i,j) - Q_L(\mathcal{I}(i,j))$;

    // Generate H
5 Losslessly compress $r_L(\mathcal{I})$ into bitstream $r_L^C(\mathcal{I})$;
6 Binary sequence $h_0 h_1 h_2 \cdots = \mathcal{W} \, \| \, r_L^C(\mathcal{I})$;   // Concatenate binary bitstreams $\mathcal{W}$ and $r_L^C(\mathcal{I})$
7 Set $H = .h_0 h_1 h_2 \cdots$ such that $H \in [0, 1)$ since each of $h_0, h_1, h_2, \cdots$ is a binary bit;

    // Convert payload to L-ary symbols and embed
8 Initialize interval $R = [0,1)$;
9 **for** $i = 1$ **to** m **do**
10   **for** $j = 1$ **to** n **do**
11       $N_L = min(\, L, 2^b - 1 - Q_L(\mathcal{I}(i,j)) \,)$;   // N_L represents the numbers of levels
                                                        // available for data embedding into $\mathcal{I}(i,j)$
12   Divide R into N_L equal sub intervals R_0 to $R_{N_L - 1}$;
13   Select sub interval R_S such that $H \in R_S$ where integer $\mathcal{S} \in [0, N_L - 1]$;
14       $\mathcal{I}'(i,j) = Q_L(\mathcal{I}(i,j)) + \mathcal{S}$;   // Embed next L-ary symbol $\mathcal{S}$ into $\mathcal{I}(i,j)$
15       $R = R_S$;

(step 9), from which the sub interval R_S is chosen so that $\mathcal{S}$ is equal to the (i,j)th quantization remainder $r_L(\mathcal{I}'(i,j))$ (steps 10–11). After each iteration corresponding to one pixel of $\mathcal{I}'$, the interval R is reset, hence narrowed down to the last value of R_S. H is recovered as nothing but the shortest bitstream belonging to the final interval R, obtained after all iterations (of *for loops* in steps 6–7) are over.

    Finally, to extract the watermark and retrieve the original cover image, we separate H into the two bitstreams (steps 13–14). First we extract the portion of H representing the original watermark $\mathcal{W}$. The remaining portion of H is decompressed (step 15) to obtain a sequence of L-ary quantization remainders, $r_L(\mathcal{I}')$. Note here that $r_L(\mathcal{I}')$ represents nothing but the sequence of original L-ary quantization remainders $r_L(\mathcal{I})$. Also the quantized watermarked image $Q_L(\mathcal{I}')$, is same as the

Procedure 4: DATA_COMPRESSION_EXTRACT

Input: Watermarked image $\mathcal{I}'$ of size $m \times n$ pixels represented by b bits each;
Output: Retrieved cover image $\mathcal{I}$; Extracted watermark $\mathcal{W}$ in form of binary bitstream;

```
// Quantize watermarked image
```
1   **for** $i = 1$ **to** m **do**
2   **for** $j = 1$ **to** n **do**
3        $Q_L(\mathcal{I}'(i, j)) = L \left\lfloor \frac{\mathcal{I}'(i,j)}{L} \right\rfloor$;   `// I'(i, j) represents the (i, j)-th pixel of I'`
4        $r_L(\mathcal{I}'(i, j)) = \mathcal{I}'(i, j) - Q_L(\mathcal{I}'(i, j))$;

```
// Recover H
```
5   Initialize interval $R = [0,1)$;
6   **for** $i = 1$ **to** m **do**
7   **for** $j = 1$ **to** n **do**
8        $N_L = min(L, 2^b - 1 - Q_L(\mathcal{I}'(i, j)))$;   `// N_L represents the numbers of levels`
                                                  `// available for data embedding into I'(i, j)`
9   Divide R into N_L equal sub intervals R_0 to R_{N_L-1};
10       $S = r_L(\mathcal{I}'(i, j))$;
11       $R = R_S$;
12   H = the shortest bitstream $\in R$;

```
// Extract watermark and retrieve cover image
```
13   Extract watermark $\mathcal{W}$ from H;
14    $r_L^C(\mathcal{I}') =$ portion of H remaining after watermark extraction;
15   Decompress $r_L^C(\mathcal{I}')$ into L-ary quantization remainders $r_L(\mathcal{I}')$;   `// Restore original remainders`
16   **for** $i = 1$ **to** m **do**
17   **for** $j = 1$ **to** n **do**
18        $\mathcal{I}(i, j) = Q_L(\mathcal{I}'(i, j)) + r_L(\mathcal{I}'(i, j))$;   `// Restore original cover image pixels`

quantized original cover image $Q_L(\mathcal{I})$. Hence, combining the restored remainders $r_L(\mathcal{I}')$ with the quantized watermarked image $Q_L(\mathcal{I}')$ retrieves the original cover image bit-by-bit (steps 16–18).

3.4   HISTOGRAM-BIN-SHIFTING

Histogram-bin-shifting technique utilizes the frequency distribution of the grayscale pixel values of an image to hide the watermark. Algorithms belonging to this class include [20, 21, 22, 23], among which we discuss Ni et al.'s [20] algorithm next.

Procedure 5: HSB_EMBED

Input: Original cover image $\mathcal{I}$ of size $m \times n$ pixels represented by b bits each; Watermark $\mathcal{W}$;
Output: Watermarked image;

    // Find *mode* of the pixel frequency histogram
1   Initialize all elements of array $count[0 .. 2^b - 1]$ to zero;
2   **for** $i = 1$ **to** m **do**
3   **for** $j = 1$ **to** n **do**
4          $count[\mathcal{I}(i, j)] = count[\mathcal{I}(i, j)] + 1;$ // $\mathcal{I}(i, j)$ represents the (i, j)-th pixel of $\mathcal{I}$
5   Initialize $peak\_frequency = count[0], peak = 0;$
6   **for** $i = 1$ **to** $2^b - 1$ **do**
7   **if** $count[i] > peak\_frequency$ **then**
8          $peak = i;$
9          $peak\_frequency = count[i];$

    // Embed $\mathcal{W}$ into $\mathcal{I}$
10 **for** $i = 1$ **to** m **do**
11   **for** $j = 1$ **to** n **do**
12   **if** $\mathcal{I}(i, j) > peak$ **then**
13            $\mathcal{I}(i, j) = \mathcal{I}(i, j) + 1;$
14   **else if** $\mathcal{I}(i, j) == peak$ **then**
15            $\mathcal{I}(i, j) = \mathcal{I}(i, j) +$ (next element of $\mathcal{W}$);   // Embed

---

Embedding Algorithm

The embedding algorithm is presented in Procedure 5 (**HSB_EMBED**). In the histogram-bin-shifting technique, the statistical *mode* of the distribution (i.e., the most frequently occurring grayscale value) is determined from the frequency histogram of the pixel values, and this particular pixel value is called the *peak value* (Fig. 3.1(a)). All the grayscale values greater than the peak value are shifted one bin to the right, so that the bin just next to the peak value is now empty. Now, the image pixels are scanned in a sequential order. To each pixel with peak grayscale value, the next watermark bit is added. As a result, when the watermark bit is a "1", the watermarked pixel will occupy the bin just emptied. Embedding capacity in such algorithms is limited by the number of pixels having the peak grayscale value. The stages of histogram modification throughout the embedding procedure is shown in Fig. 3.1 for standard grayscale test image, 512×512 *Lena*.

Extraction Algorithm

For extraction (Procedure 6 (**HSB_EXTRACT**)), the watermarked image is scanned in the same sequential order. Whenever a pixel with the previous peak grayscale value (i.e., the grayscale value

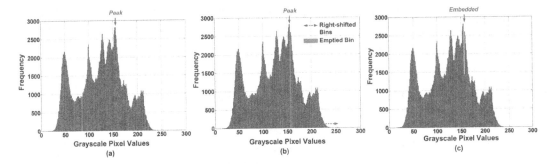

FIGURE 3.1: Pixel frequency histogram-bin-shifting of 512×512 grayscale *Lena* image: (a) histogram showing frequency distribution of grayscale pixel values; (b) bin just next to the peak value is emptied; and (c) histogram after watermark embedding.

Procedure 6: HSB_EXTRACT

Input: Watermarked image $\mathcal{I}_W$ of size $m \times n$ pixels represented by b bits each; *peak* (mode of histogram);
Output: Retrieved cover image; Extracted watermark;

1 Initialize *counter* $= 0$;
2 **for** $i = 1$ **to** m **do**
3   **for** $j = 1$ **to** n **do**
4   **if** $\mathcal{I}_W(i, j) > peak + 1$ **then**   // $\mathcal{I}_W(i, j)$ represents the (i, j)-th pixel of $\mathcal{I}_W$
5   Restore $\mathcal{I}_W(i, j) = \mathcal{I}_W(i, j) - 1$;
6   **else if** $\mathcal{I}(i, j) == peak + 1$ **then**
7   Restore $\mathcal{I}_W(i, j) = \mathcal{I}_W(i, j) - 1$;
8   Extract next watermark bit '0';
9   **else if** $\mathcal{I}(i, j) == peak$ **then**
10   Extract next watermark bit '1';

with maximum frequency before watermark embedding) is encountered, it is inferred that the watermark bit embedded in that pixel was "0". However, if a pixel whose value is one more than the previous peak grayscale value is encountered, it is inferred that the watermark bit embedded in that pixel was "1" and we subtract this "1" from the pixel value. Finally, each pixel greater than (*peak_grayscale_value* + 1), gets one subtracted from its value. Therefore, the histograms of such pixels are now left shifted by one bin, which restores back the original cover image.

Procedure 7: CIRCULAR_HSB_EMBED

Input: Original cover image $\mathcal{I}$; Watermark $\mathcal{W}$;
Output: Watermarked image;

1 **foreach** pixel group of $\mathcal{I}$ **do**
2   **if** principal axes of zones A and B are oriented in the same direction **then**
            `// This group is suitable for watermark embedding`
3   **if** next watermark bit is '1' **then** apply circular, clockwise shift to the principal axis of A;
4   **else** apply circular, anti-clockwise shift to the principal axis of A;

3.4.1   CIRCULAR HISTOGRAM-BIN-SHIFTING

Another histogram-bin-shifting–based reversible watermarking algorithm was proposed by Vlees-chouwer et al. [22], [23] where pixel frequency histograms are circularly interpreted. A *group* of pixels is used to embed each watermark bit. Each group is randomly divided into two equal sized *zones*, A and B. To embed a watermark bit, the histogram of zone B is kept unmodified, whereas the histogram bins of zone A are circularly shifted clockwise (to embed a "1") or anti-clockwise (to embed a "0"). The pixels of each zone is mapped to a circle, whose principal axis represents the center of mass of the circle, i.e., the axis from the center of the circle to the point on the circle corresponding to the mode of the zone's frequency histogram. The correctness of this scheme depends on the fact that it is highly probable that the principal axes of the original (unwatermarked) zones A and B are closely oriented, since the zones are generated randomly from a group of pixels and both zones consist of an equal number of pixels. For watermark extraction, the relative orientation of the principal axes of zones A and B is checked for each group of pixels in the watermarked image. If the principal axis of A is found to be shifted clockwise (anti-clockwise), the watermark bit extracted is a "1" ("0") and a subsequent anti-clockwise (clockwise) shift of A's principal axis restores the pixels to their original values, facilitating reversibility. The reversible watermarking algorithm embedding and extraction algorithms of Vleeschouwer et al. [22] are presented in Procedures 7 (**CIRCULAR_HSB_EMBED**) and 8 (**CIRCULAR_HSB_EXTRACT**) respectively.

The technique of histogram-bin-shifting for reversible watermarking, is not restricted in its applicability to the grayscale pixel values. In fact, it is a general technique which is applied widely to transformed domain image parameters, to achieve reversibility. For example, in Section 3.5 we shall discuss a technique of reversible watermarking, where a pixel is predicted based on its neighborhood and the image is reversibly watermarked by modification of prediction error. Now, here modification

Procedure 8: CIRCULAR_HSB_EXTRACT

Input: Watermarked image $\mathcal{I}_W$;
Output: Retrieved cover image; Extracted watermark;

1 **foreach** pixel group of $\mathcal{I}_W$ **do**
2   **if** this was a suitable group for watermark embedding **then**
3   **if** principal axis of A is circularly clockwise shifted w.r.t. principal axis of B **then**
4   Extract next watermark bit '1';
5   Apply circular, anti-clockwise shift to the principal axis of A;
6   **else if** principal axis of A is circularly anti-clockwise shifted w.r.t. principal axis of B **then**
7   Extract next watermark bit '0';
8   Apply circular, clockwise shift to the principal axis of A;

of prediction error is nothing but modification of error histogram in effect. This will be clearer from our discussion in Section 3.5.

3.5   PIXEL PREDICTION

In this class of reversible watermarking algorithms [5, 9, 25, 26, 27], some of the cover image pixels are predicted based on their neighboring pixels. Such prediction gives rise to predicted pixel values as well as prediction errors. The watermark symbols (bits) are embedded into the prediction errors. The modified errors and the predicted pixels are combined to produce the watermarked image. As mentioned previously, this class constitutes the most widely studied state-of-the-art reversible watermarking algorithms. Luo et al.'s [5] pixel prediction-based reversible watermarking technique will be described next, as the representative example.

Embedding Algorithm

Luo et al.'s [5] prediction based reversible watermark embedding algorithm is presented in Procedure 9 (**PREDICTION_EMBED**) [5]. The user selects certain pixel locations within the cover image to embed watermark bits (step 2). Within this set, each pixel is predicted as the mean of its four neighbors (steps 3–4) and the prediction error is computed for each pixel (step 5). To embed the watermark W into the cover image $\mathcal{I}$, a thresholding technique is applied. Only those prediction errors whose absolute values do not exceed the threshold $\mathcal{T}$ are used for embedding (steps 9–10). This technique helps to achieve optimal distortion of the watermarked image. A constant shift of magnitude $(\mathcal{T} + 1)$ is applied to the prediction errors exceeding the threshold (steps 11–12), to

---

Procedure 9: PREDICTION_EMBED

Input: Original cover image $\mathcal{I}$ of size $m \times n$ pixels; Watermark $\mathcal{W}$; Threshold $\mathcal{T}$;
Output: Watermarked image $\mathcal{I}'$;

1 Initialize $\mathcal{I}' = \mathcal{I}$;

   `// Perform pixel prediction`

2 Select some pixel locations (i, j) for embedding where $1 \leq i \leq m$ and $1 \leq j \leq n$;

3 **if** $(i, j) \in$ Set of pixel locations selected for embedding **then**

4   Predict $\mathcal{I}'(i, j) =$ Mean of four neighbors of $\mathcal{I}(i, j)$;   `// ` $\mathcal{I}(i, j)$ ` represents the`
                                                                        `// ` (i, j)`-th pixel of ` $\mathcal{I}$

5 Compute prediction error matrix $e = \mathcal{I} - \mathcal{I}'$;

   `// Embed watermark`

6 **for** $i = 1$ **to** m **do**

7   **for** $j = 1$ **to** n **do**

8   **if** $(i, j) \in$ Set of pixel locations selected for embedding **then**

9   **if** $|e(i, j)| <= \mathcal{T}$ **then**   `// Embed`

10                 $e'(i, j) = sign(\,e(i, j)\,) \times (\,2 \times |e(i, j)| + b\,)$, where $b \in [0, 1]$;

11   **else if** $|e(i, j)| > \mathcal{T}$ **then**   `// Apply constant shift`

12                 $e'(i, j) = sign(\,e(i, j)\,) \times (\,|e(i, j)| + \mathcal{T} + 1\,)$;

13             $\mathcal{I}'(i, j) = \mathcal{I}'(i, j) + e'(i, j)$;

---

avoid any possible overlap of modified prediction errors. Finally, the modified prediction errors are combined with the predicted pixels in step 13.

Note here that, in pixel prediction-based reversible watermark embedding algorithm, the technique of histogram-bin-shifting is applied to the prediction error frequency histogram. Modification of the prediction error histogram due to watermark embedding is depicted by an example, in Fig. 3.2.

Extraction Algorithm

Luo et al.'s [5] prediction-based reversible watermark extraction algorithm is presented in Procedure 10 (**PREDICTION_EXTRACT**), where it is assumed that the extractor has the knowledge regarding the pixel locations selected by the embedder [5]. A pixel belonging to this set is predicted as the mean of its four neighbors and the prediction error is computed for each pixel (step 2–4). The LSBs of the prediction errors obtained from the watermarked pixels represent nothing but the embedded watermark bits. In the embedding algorithm the watermark bits were embedded into those prediction errors which had absolute values less than or equal to the threshold $\mathcal{T}$. So, the watermark

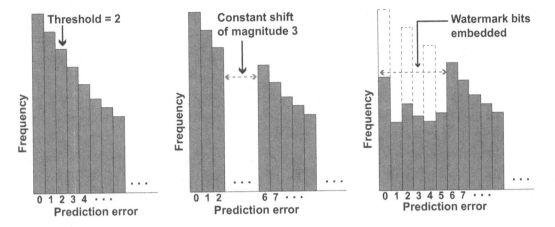

FIGURE 3.2: Steps of prediction error histogram modification for watermark embedding.

Procedure 10: PREDICTION_EXTRACT

Input: Watermarked image $\mathcal{I}'$ of size $m \times n$ pixels; Threshold $\mathcal{T}$;
Output: Retrieved cover image $\mathcal{I}$; Extracted watermark;

1   Initialize $\mathcal{I} = \mathcal{I}'$;
    // Perform pixel prediction
2   **if** $(i, j) \in$ Set of pixel locations selected for embedding **then**
3   Predict $\mathcal{I}(i, j) =$ Mean of four neighbors of $\mathcal{I}'(i, j)$;
4   Compute prediction error matrix $e' = \mathcal{I}' - \mathcal{I}$;

    // Extract watermark
5   **for** $i = 1$ **to** m **do**
6   **for** $j = 1$ **to** n **do**
7   **if** $(i, j) \in$ Set of pixel locations selected for embedding **then**
8   **if** $|e'(i, j)| <= (2\mathcal{T} + 1)$ **then**   // Extract
9   Extract next watermark bit $= mod(e'(i, j), 2)$;
10          $e(i, j) = \left\lfloor \frac{e'(i, j)}{2} \right\rfloor$;
11   **else if** $|e'(i, j)| > (2\mathcal{T} + 1)$ **then**   // Apply reverse constant shift
12          $e(i, j) = sign(e'(i, j)) \times (|e'(i, j)| - \mathcal{T} - 1)$;
13         $\mathcal{I}(i, j) = \mathcal{I}(i, j) + e(i, j)$;

bits are extracted only from those prediction errors whose absolute values do not exceed $(2\mathcal{T}+1)$; subsequently the prediction errors are restored back to their original forms by one bit right shifting (steps 8–10). The rest of the prediction errors are shifted back to their original magnitudes by a constant $-(\mathcal{T}+1)$, in steps 11–12. Finally, the restored prediction errors are combined with the predicted pixels (step 13), which restores the original cover image $\mathcal{I}$.

To avoid pixel overflow, the prediction-based reversible watermarking technique makes use of the *location map*. In the extraction algorithm of Procedure 10, the *location map* is extracted from the LSBs of the watermarked image marginal pixels, in step 10. A *location map* bit set to "0" indicates that the corresponding pixel was not used for embedding since it was capable of causing an overflow, whereas a *location map* bit set to "1" indicates that the corresponding pixel location has a watermark bit embedded. During extraction, only those prediction errors were modified, corresponding to which the *location map* bits were set to "1" (steps 19–21,30–31). The prediction errors corresponding to which the *location map* bits were set to "0", were kept unmodified throughout the procedure (steps 17–18,28–29). Procedure 10 extracts the watermark and restores the original cover image without any bit loss.

3.5.1 A RECENT REVERSIBLE DATA HIDING TECHNIQUE BASED ON PIXEL PREDICTION

Recently Li et al. [24] proposed a reversible watermarking scheme using an efficient pixel prediction technique with improved accuracy. This algorithm operates on consecutive pixel pairs of an image. The embedding locations are decided depending on the difference of the two pixels as well as their predicted values.

The reversible watermark embedding algorithm proposed by Li et al. [24] for 8-bit images is presented in Procedure 11. In Procedure 11, the difference between a pair of adjacent pixels is computed as d_1 in step 3. The second pixel of a pair is predicted in steps 4–13 and the prediction error d_2 is computed in step 14. Depending on the range of d_1, d_2 values, the watermark bit "0" or "1" is embedded into the pixel pair (steps 15–19). The pixel pairs which are not used for embedding are shifted by constant 1 in order to avoid any possible overlap of grayscale values (steps 20–23).

Li et al.'s [24] reversible watermark extraction algorithm is presented in Procedure 12. Similar to the embedding procedure, during extraction the difference between each pair of adjacent (watermarked) pixels is computed as d_1 in step 3 and the second pixel of the pair is predicted in steps 4–13, followed by the prediction error (d_2) computation in step 14. Depending on the range of d_1, d_2 values, the embedded watermark bit is extracted from a pixel pair along with original pixel restoration (steps 15–35). The pixel pairs without any embedded watermark bit are shifted back to their original values in steps 36–39.

Procedure 11: DIFF_PREDICTION_EMBED

Input: Original 8-bit cover image $\mathcal{I}$ of size $m \times n$ pixels; Watermark $\mathcal{W}$;
Output: Watermarked image $\mathcal{I}'$;

1 Initialize $\mathcal{I}' = \mathcal{I}$;
2 **foreach** consecutive pixel pair $(\mathcal{I}(i, j), \mathcal{I}(i, j+1))$ of $\mathcal{I}$ **do**
3   Compute difference $d_1 = \mathcal{I}(i, j) - \mathcal{I}(i, j+1)$;
    // Predict $\mathcal{I}(i, j+1)$ as z
4      $d_v = |\mathcal{I}(i, j+2) - \mathcal{I}(i+1, j+2)| + |\mathcal{I}(i+1, j) - \mathcal{I}(i+2, j)|$
    $+|\mathcal{I}(i+1, j+1) - \mathcal{I}(i+2, j+1)|$;
5      $d_h = |\mathcal{I}(i, j+2) - \mathcal{I}(i, j+3)| + |\mathcal{I}(i+1, j) - \mathcal{I}(i+1, j+1)|$
    $+|\mathcal{I}(i+1, j+1) - \mathcal{I}(i+1, j+2)|$;
6      $u = \frac{\mathcal{I}(i, j+2) + \mathcal{I}(i+1, j+1)}{2} + \frac{\mathcal{I}(i+1, j) - \mathcal{I}(i+1, j+2)}{2}$;
7   **if** $d_v - d_h > 80$ **then** $z = \mathcal{I}(i, j+2)$;
8   **else if** $d_v - d_h \in (32, 80]$ **then** $z = \frac{\mathcal{I}(i, j+2) + u}{2}$;
9   **else if** $d_v - d_h \in (8, 32]$ **then** $z = \frac{\mathcal{I}(i, j+2) + 3u}{4}$;
10   **else if** $d_v - d_h \in [-8, 8]$ **then** $z = u$;
11   **else if** $d_v - d_h \in [-32, -8)$ **then** $z = \frac{\mathcal{I}(i+1, j+1) + 3u}{4}$;
12   **else if** $d_v - d_h \in [-80, -32)$ **then** $z = \frac{\mathcal{I}(i+1, j+1) + u}{2}$;
13   **else if** $d_v - d_h < -80$ **then** $z = \mathcal{I}(i+1, j+1)$;
14   Compute prediction error $d_2 = I(i, j+1) - z$;
    // Embed next watermark symbol $b \in 0, 1$ or Right Shift
15   **if** $d_1 = 1 \,\&\&\, d_2 > 0$ **then** $\mathcal{I}'(i, j) = \mathcal{I}(i, j) + b$;
16   **else if** $d_1 = -1 \,\&\&\, d_2 < 0$ **then** $\mathcal{I}'(i, j) = \mathcal{I}(i, j) - b$;
17   **else if** $(d_1 = 0 \,\&\&\, d_2 \geq 0) \,||\, (d_1 < 0 \,\&\&\, d_2 = 0)$ **then** $\mathcal{I}'(i, j+1) = \mathcal{I}(i, j+1) + b$;
18   **else if** $(d_1 = 0 \,\&\&\, d_2 < 0) \,||\, (d_1 > 0 \,\&\&\, d_2 = 0) \,||\, (d_1 = 1 \,\&\&\, d_2 = -1)$ **then**
19         $\mathcal{I}'(i, j+1) = \mathcal{I}(i, j+1) - b$;
20   **else if** $d_1 > 1 \,\&\&\, d_2 > 0$ **then** $\mathcal{I}'(i, j) = \mathcal{I}(i, j) + 1$;
21   **else if** $d_1 < -1 \,\&\&\, d_2 < 0$ **then** $\mathcal{I}'(i, j) = \mathcal{I}(i, j) - 1$;
22   **else if** $d_1 < 0 \,\&\&\, d_2 > 0$ **then** $\mathcal{I}'(i, j+1) = \mathcal{I}(i, j+1) + 1$;
23   **else if** $d_1 = 1 \,\&\&\, d_2 < -1$ **then** $\mathcal{I}'(i, j+1) = \mathcal{I}(i, j+1) - 1$;

Note that in Li et al.'s algorithm, the shift in grayscale value due to watermark embedding is applied to either of the two pixels in a pair. If we consider each pixel pair to be a point in a two-dimensional space then due to embedding, each such point is shifted left, right, up or down.

Procedure 12: DIFF_PREDICTION_EXTRACT

Input: 8-bit watermarked image $\mathcal{I}'$ of size $m \times n$ pixels;
Output: Retrieved cover image $\mathcal{I}$; Extracted watermark;

1   Initialize $\mathcal{I} = \mathcal{I}'$;
2   **foreach** consecutive pixel pair $(\mathcal{I}'(i, j), \mathcal{I}'(i, j+1))$ of $\mathcal{I}'$ **do**
3   Compute difference $d_1 = \mathcal{I}'(i, j) - \mathcal{I}'(i, j+1)$;
       // Predict $\mathcal{I}'(i, j+1)$ as z
4       $d_v = |\mathcal{I}'(i, j+2) - \mathcal{I}'(i+1, j+2)| + |\mathcal{I}'(i+1, j) - \mathcal{I}'(i+2, j)| + |\mathcal{I}'(i+1, j+1) - \mathcal{I}'(i+2, j+1)|$;
5       $d_h = |\mathcal{I}'(i, j+2) - \mathcal{I}'(i, j+3)| + |\mathcal{I}'(i+1, j) - \mathcal{I}'(i+1, j+1)| + |\mathcal{I}'(i+1, j+1) - \mathcal{I}'(i+1, j+2)|$;
6       $u = \frac{\mathcal{I}'(i, j+2) + \mathcal{I}'(i+1, j+1)}{2} + \frac{\mathcal{I}'(i+1, j) - \mathcal{I}'(i+1, j+2)}{2}$;
7   **if** $d_v - d_h > 80$ **then** $z = \mathcal{I}'(i, j+2)$;
8   **else if** $d_v - d_h \in (32, 80]$ **then** $z = \frac{\mathcal{I}'(i, j+2) + u}{2}$;
9   **else if** $d_v - d_h \in (8, 32]$ **then** $z = \frac{\mathcal{I}'(i, j+2) + 3u}{4}$;
10   **else if** $d_v - d_h \in [-8, 8]$ **then** $z = u$;
11   **else if** $d_v - d_h \in [-32, -8)$ **then** $z = \frac{\mathcal{I}'(i+1, j+1) + 3u}{4}$;
12   **else if** $d_v - d_h \in [-80, -32)$ **then** $z = \frac{\mathcal{I}'(i+1, j+1) + u}{2}$;
13   **else if** $d_v - d_h < -80$ **then** $z = \mathcal{I}'(i+1, j+1)$;
14   Compute prediction error $d_2 = I'(i, j+1) - z$;
       // Extract next watermark symbol $b \in 0, 1$ and restore pixel
15   **if** $d_1 \in \{1, 2\}$ && $d_2 > 0$ **then**
16          $b = d_1 - 1$;
17          $\mathcal{I}(i, j) = \mathcal{I}'(i, j) - b$;
18   **else if** $d_1 \in \{-1, -2\}$ && $d_2 < 0$ **then**
19          $b = -1 - d_1$;
20          $\mathcal{I}(i, j) = \mathcal{I}'(i, j) + b$;
21   **else if** $(d_1 = 0$ && $d_2 \geq 0)$ || $(d_1 = -1$ && $d_2 \geq 1)$ **then**
22          $b = -d_1$;
23          $\mathcal{I}(i, j+1) = \mathcal{I}'(i, j+1) - b$;
24   **else if** $(d_1 < 0$ && $d_2 = 0)$ || $(d_1 < -1$ && $d_2 = 1)$ **then**
25          $b = d_2$;
26          $\mathcal{I}(i, j+1) = \mathcal{I}'(i, j+1) - b$;
27   **else if** $(d_1 = 0$ && $d_2 < 0)$ || $(d_1 = 1$ && $d_2 < -1)$ **then**
28          $b = d_1$;
29          $\mathcal{I}'(i, j+1) = \mathcal{I}(i, j+1) + b$;
30   **else if** $(d_1 > 0$ && $d_2 = 0)$ || $(d_1 > 1$ && $d_2 = -1)$ **then**
31          $b = -d_2$;
32          $\mathcal{I}'(i, j+1) = \mathcal{I}(i, j+1) + b$;
33   **else if** $(d_1 = 1$ && $d_2 = -1)$ || $(d_1 = 2$ && $d_2 = -2)$ **then**
34          $b = d_1 - 1$;
35          $\mathcal{I}'(i, j+1) = \mathcal{I}(i, j+1) + b$;
36   **else if** $d_1 > 2$ && $d_2 > 0$ **then** $\mathcal{I}(i, j) = \mathcal{I}'(i, j) - 1$;
37   **else if** $d_1 < -2$ && $d_2 < 0$ **then** $\mathcal{I}(i, j) = \mathcal{I}'(i, j) + 1$;
38   **else if** $d_1 < -1$ && $d_2 > 1$ **then** $\mathcal{I}(i, j+1) = \mathcal{I}'(i, j+1) - 1$;
39   **else if** $(d_1 > 2$ && $d_2 < -1)$ || $(d_1 = 2$ && $d_2 < -2)$ **then** $\mathcal{I}(i, j+1) = \mathcal{I}'(i, j+1) + 1$;

Procedure 13: IDCT_EMBED

Input: Original cover image $\mathcal{I}$ of size $m \times n$ pixels; Watermark $\mathcal{W}$; Set of locations within
     an 8×8 block selected for embedding;
Output: Watermarked image $\mathcal{I}'$;

1 **for** $i = 1$ **to** $\frac{m}{8}$ **do**
2   **for** $j = 1$ **to** $\frac{n}{8}$ **do**
          // Watermark individual 8×8 blocks of $\mathcal{I}$
3        $x_{i,j} = \mathcal{I}(8i - 7 : 8i,\ 8j - 7 : 8j)$;   // $\mathcal{I}(i_1 : i_2, j_1 : j_2)$ represents a pixel submatrix of $\mathcal{I}$
4        $\mathcal{X}_{i,j} = $ IDCT of $x_{i,j}$;
5   **for** $k = 1$ **to** 8 **do**
6   **for** $l = 1$ **to** 8 **do**
7   **if** (k, l) belongs to set of selected embedding locations of an 8×8 block **then**
                 // Left shift and embed
8                 $\mathcal{X}_{i,j}(k, l) = 2 \times \mathcal{X}_{i,j}(k, l) + $ (next element of $\mathcal{W}$);
9        $\mathcal{I}'(8i - 7 : 8i,\ 8j - 7 : 8j) = $ Inverse IDCT of $\mathcal{X}_{i,j}$;

3.6   MODIFICATION OF FREQUENCY DOMAIN CHARACTERISTICS

In this class of reversible watermarking algorithms [6] the watermark is embedded into the frequency domain representation of the cover image. Here we discuss the reversible watermarking algorithm proposed by Yang et al. [6], which uses the *Integer Discrete Cosine Transform* (IDCT) characteristics of the cover image, for watermark embedding. The IDCT, originally proposed by Plonka and Tasche in [28], is a completely invertible integer-to-integer transform.

Embedding Algorithm

The reversible watermark embedding algorithm based on modification of IDCT characteristics of an image is presented in Procedure 13 (**IDCT_EMBED**). In this technique, 8×8 pixel submatrix ($x_{i,j}$) of the cover image $\mathcal{I}$ are considered for watermark embedding, individually (*for loops* of steps 1–2). Invertible IDCT [28] is applied to each 8×8 block $x_{i,j}$ (steps 3–4), producing another 8×8 block $\mathcal{X}_{i,j}$, representing the IDCT coefficients of $x_{i,j}$.

In this class of reversible watermarking algorithms, some locations within an 8×8 block are selected a priori by the user which are to be used for embedding watermark bits. In Procedure 13, the watermark bits are embedded into the selected locations of each 8×8 IDCT coefficients block in steps 5–8. To embed a watermark bit into the (k, l)–th element of the 8×8 IDCT coefficients block $\mathcal{X}_{i,j}$, the element is left shifted by one bit and the watermark bit is inserted into its LSB position

Procedure 14: IDCT_EXTRACT

Input: Watermarked image $\mathcal{I}'$ of size $m \times n$ pixels; Set of locations within an 8×8 block
     selected for embedding;

Output: Retrieved cover image $\mathcal{I}$; Watermark $\mathcal{W}$;

1   **for** $i = 1$ **to** $\frac{m}{8}$ **do**
2   **for** $j = 1$ **to** $\frac{n}{8}$ **do**
       // Retrieve individual 8×8 blocks of $\mathcal{I}$
3        $x'_{i,j} = \mathcal{I}'(8i - 7 : 8i,\ 8j - 7 : 8j)$;   // $\mathcal{I}(i, j)$ represents the (i, j)-th pixel of $\mathcal{I}'$
4        $\mathcal{X}_{i,j} = \text{IDCT of } x'_{i,j}$;
5   **for** $k = 1$ **to** 8 **do**
6   **for** $l = 1$ **to** 8 **do**
7   **if** (k, l) belongs to set of selected embedding locations of an 8×8 block **then**
8   Extract next element of $\mathcal{W} = mod(\mathcal{X}_{i,j}(k, l), 2)$;
9   Restore $\mathcal{X}_{i,j}(k, l) = \left\lfloor \frac{\mathcal{X}_{i,j}(k,l)}{2} \right\rfloor$;
10   Retrieve $\mathcal{I}(8i - 7 : 8i,\ 8j - 7 : 8j)$ = Inverse IDCT of $\mathcal{X}_{i,j}$;

(step 8). Finally, the *inverse* IDCT is applied to each modified 8×8 IDCT coefficients block to produce the corresponding 8×8 watermarked image block (step 9). The entire above procedure is repeated for all 8×8 blocks of the cover image.

Extraction Algorithm

The reversible watermark extraction algorithm based on cover image IDCT coefficients modification is presented in Procedure 14 (**IDCT_EXTRACT**). In the extraction algorithm, each 8×8 block of the watermarked image is restored to its original form individually, and watermark bits are extracted from it. IDCT is applied to each 8×8 block $x'_{i,j}$ of the watermarked image $\mathcal{I}'$, to produce 8×8 block of its IDCT coefficients $\mathcal{X}_{i,j}$ (steps 3–4).

Within each 8×8 IDCT coefficients block, watermark bits are extracted from the LSB positions of those elements, which belong to the set of locations originally selected for watermark embedding (step 8); subsequently, the element is restored back to its original form by one bit right shifting (step 9).

Finally, the *inverse* IDCT is applied to each restored 8×8 IDCT coefficients block to retrieve the corresponding 8×8 original cover image block (step 10). The entire procedure is repeated for all 8×8 blocks to restore the entire original image.

In the above discussion we presented a overview of the five classes of reversible watermarking algorithms, by a representative example from each class. In the next section, we discuss in detail the operation and performance of a very recently developed reversible watermarking technique for digital images.

3.7 SUMMARY

In this chapter we discussed five major techniques of reversible watermarking techniques. A particular state-of-the-art reversible watermarking algorithm may utilize one or more of the techniques discussed. Also, there may be overlap between the operating principles of two or more techniques discussed in this chapter.

As is evident from our discussion in this chapter, a number of mathematically and computationally complex steps are involved in the implementation of reversible watermarking algorithms, mainly due to the demands imposed by the reversibility property. Specifically, the following operations involve the above-mentioned complex steps: (1) invertible integer transforms such as IDCT (e.g. Procedures 13–14); (2) lossless compression and decompression algorithms (e.g. Procedures 1, 2, 3, 4); (3) some operations such as computing the location map (e.g., Sections 3.2 and 3.5), creation of pixel frequency histogram (e.g., Procedures 5–8) also make the reversible watermarking algorithms computationally more complex compared to their non-reversible counterparts. However, in the existing literature the conventional parameters widely used by researchers for evaluation and comparison of those algorithms are *watermark embedding capacity*, *watermarked image distortion* and *distorion vs. capacity* characteristics.

In the next chapter we will present the detailed working of a reversible watermarking algorithm, to give the readers a clearer idea of the operational steps of a reversible watermarking technique.

CHAPTER 4

Detailed Working of a Reversible Watermarking Algorithm: A Technique Utilizing Weighted Median-Based Prediction

4.1 INTRODUCTION

In this chapter we describe in details the working of a reversible watermarking algorithm with the help of an example. In general, reversible watermarking of digital images is carried out by exploiting the high spatial correlation among neighboring pixels. A feature of the cover image is selected, which is modified to embed the watermark bits. For example, the grayscale values of pixels, the difference of adjacent pixels' grayscale values, the quantization or interpolation errors after the pixels are quantized or interpolated, respectively, are some of the features selected by various authors.

In this chapter, we discuss the detailed operation of a pixel prediction-based reversible watermarking algorithm, recently published [25]. Our algorithm exploits spatial correlation among neighboring pixels of an image to predict the grayscale values of the pixel. We considered the median of a group of pixels for predicting the value of their common neighboring pixel. To enhance the accuracy of the prediction process, we assigned weights to the neighboring pixel values during the prediction, and then calculated a *weighted median* (details of the weight assignment scheme is in Section 4.2.2). Difference of pixel values with their predicted values are then modified for embedding the watermark.

We describe the watermark embedding algorithm in Section 4.2 and the watermark extraction algorithm in Section 4.3. The experimental results demonstrating the performance of the algorithm are presented in Section 4.6. Finally, we summarize the chapter in Section 4.7.

4.2 WATERMARK EMBEDDING ALGORITHM

The algorithm [25] utilizes the spatial correlation among neighboring pixel values in grayscale images. It predicts the grayscale value of a pixel from those of its neighboring pixels and the

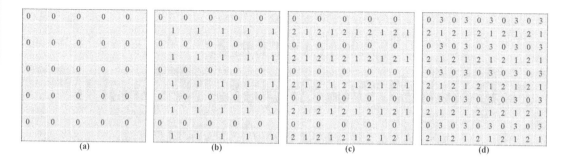

FIGURE 4.1: Locations of (a) base pixels ("0"s); (b) predicted first set of pixels ("1"s); (c) predicted second set of pixels ("2"s); and (d) predicted third set of pixels ("3"s).

watermark bits are embedded into the prediction errors. Depending on the order, of prediction, the pixels are divided into four classes as follows.

1. The pixels of the cover image whose values remain unchanged during the watermarking process are termed *base pixels*.

2. From the base pixels, the *first set of predicted pixel values* are derived.

3. Further, the *second* and *third sets of predicted pixel values* are derived from the base pixels and first set of predicted pixel values.

Locations of the base pixels, first, second and third sets of interpolated pixels are marked with "0"s, "1"s, "2"s and "3"s, respectively, in Fig. 4.1.

Figure 4.2 shows the flowchart of our watermark embedding algorithm. Our watermark embedding algorithm consists of *four* broad steps: (a) selection of base pixels; (b) predicting other pixels from the base pixels; (c) computing the prediction errors; and (d) embedding watermark bits into the errors. We next describe the steps shown in Fig. 4.2.

4.2.1 SELECTION OF BASE PIXELS

One out of every four pixels in the original cover image is chosen as a *base pixel* in our algorithm, such that they are uniformly distributed throughout the image. The positions of the base pixels we selected in an image are marked with "0"s in Fig. 4.1.

4.2.2 PREDICTING THREE SETS OF PIXELS

To predict the grayscale value of a pixel, we compute a *weighted median* of its adjacent pixel values. Since adjacent pixels are usually highly correlated, the weighted median of neighboring pixels provides good prediction for most pixels. To compute the *median* of n integer pixel values

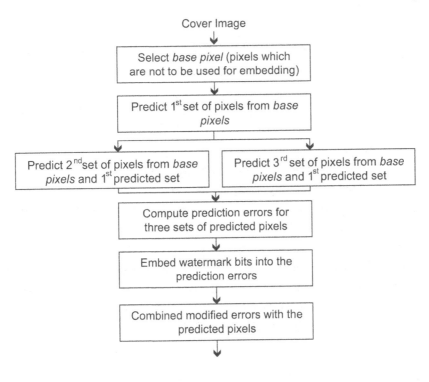

Cover Image

FIGURE 4.2: Proposed reversible watermarking algorithm.

$i_1, i_2, \ldots, i_n$, the integers are first sorted into the sequence $i_{(1)}, i_{(2)}, \ldots, i_{(n)}$, such that $i_{(1)} \leq i_{(2)} \leq \cdots \leq i_{(n)}$. Then, their median is computed as:

$$median(i_1, i_2, \ldots, i_n) = \begin{cases} i_{((n+1)/2)} & \text{if } n \text{ is odd} \\ [i_{(n/2)} + i_{(n/2+1)}]/2 & \text{otherwise.} \end{cases} \quad (4.1)$$

Weighted median of n pixel values $p_1, p_2, \ldots, p_n$ is computed as:

$$WM(\{p_1, p_2, \ldots, p_n\}, \{w_1, w_2, \ldots, w_n\}) = median(w_1 \diamond p_1, w_2 \diamond p_2, \ldots, w_n \diamond p_n), \quad (4.2)$$

where non-negative integers $w_1, w_2, \ldots, w_n$ are the weights assigned to pixels $p_1, p_2, \ldots, p_n$ respectively, and $w_i \diamond p_i$ implies w_i repetitions of pixel p_i. For example, let the grayscale values four pixels be 167, 168, 240, 255 and their assigned weights be $w_1 = 1$, $w_2 = 2$, $w_3 = 3$, $w_2 = 2$, respectively. The weighted median of the pixels will be calculated as:

$$WM(\{167, 168, 240, 255\}, \{1, 2, 3, 2\})$$

$$= median(1 \diamond 167, 2 \diamond 168, 3 \diamond 240, 2 \diamond 255)$$

$$= median(167, 168, 168, 240, 240, 240, 255, 255)$$

$$= 240.$$

In the proposed algorithm one pixel is predicted as the weighted-median of its neighboring pixels. Among the neighboring pixels, some are the original pixels whereas others are predicted pixels themselves. While computing the median, the original neighboring pixels are assigned higher weights than the predicted neighboring pixels in order to increase the accuracy of predicting, thus minimizing the absolute values of the prediction errors. The weights assigned to the original and predicted neighbors in our experiments, are in the ratio 2:1. This will be made clearer by the discussion that follows.

The first set of pixels are predicted from the base pixels whereas the second and third sets of pixels are predicted from the base pixels as well as the predicted values of the first set of pixels. Predicted value of each first-set pixel depends on the four base pixels surrounding its on its four corners, with equal weights assigned all four pixels. The prediction formula is:

$$\xi(p(i, j)) \tag{4.3}$$
$$= WM(\{p(i - 1, j - 1), p(i - 1, j + 1), p(i + 1, j - 1), p(i + 1, j + 1)\}, \{1, 1, 1, 1\}),$$

where i and j are the row and column numbers of the pixel to be predicted, respectively.

Each second-set pixel located at (i, j)th pixel position is predicted from the two base pixels located on its top $(i - 1, j)$ and bottom $(i + 1, j)$, as well as the two predicted first-set pixels located on its left $(i, j - 1)$ and right $(i, j + 1)$. We assign higher weights to the base pixels, since they are the original non-predicted pixels, and lower weights to the predicted first set of pixels. The prediction formula for a pixel $p(i, j)$ belonging to the second set is:

$$\xi(p(i, j)) = WM(\{p(i, j - 1), p(i, j + 1), p(i - 1, j), p(i + 1, j)\}, \{1, 1, 2, 2\}). \tag{4.4}$$

Prediction of the third set of pixels is similar to that of the second set. Predicted value of each third-set pixel located at (i, j)th pixel position, depends on the two base pixels located on its left $(i, j - 1)$ and right $(i, j + 1)$, as well as the two predicted first-set pixels located on its top $(i - 1, j)$ and bottom $(i + 1, j)$. Again, the base pixels are assigned higher weights than the predicted first set of pixels. The prediction formula for a pixel $p(i, j)$ belonging to the third set is:

$$\xi(p(i, j)) = WM(\{p(i, j - 1), p(i, j + 1), p(i - 1, j), p(i + 1, j)\}, \{2, 2, 1, 1\}). \tag{4.5}$$

To predict a border pixel, we assign *zero* weights to those of its neighbors which are absent. Figure 4.1(a)–(d) show the order of pixel set predictions.

4.2.3   COMPUTING PREDICTION ERRORS

Prediction error is given by the difference between an original pixel value and its prediction. For each predicted pixel we compute prediction error using the following integer transformation:

$$e = \xi(p) - p. \tag{4.6}$$

Due to high correlation of adjacent pixels, in practice, usually the errors are small integers, close to zero.

4.2.4   EMBEDDING WATERMARK BITS

Prediction errors which are close to zero are used to embed the watermark bits, leading to achievement of high embedding capacity, since the number of errors close to zero is usually large. To define *closeness to zero*, we adopt an *error threshold* k (≥ 0). Only those pixels with prediction errors $|e| \leq k$ are used for embedding watermark bits. A watermark bit is embedded into an error, by multiplying the error by 2 and adding the watermark bit to the result. For pixels with $|e| > k$, a constant shift of magnitude $(k + 1)$ is applied to the absolute prediction error values to avoid overlap with pixels in which watermark bits are embedded. Procedure 15 is followed to embed watermark bits into the prediction errors.

Procedure 15: EMBED_WATERMARK

Input: Original pixel prediction error (e), error threshold (k);
Output: Modified prediction errors $\phi(e)$;

```
// Embed watermark bits into the prediction errors
```
1   **if** $e < 0$ **then**
2        $sgn(e) \leftarrow -1$;
3   **else**
4        $sgn(e) \leftarrow +1$;
5   **if** $(|e| > k)$ **then**
6        $\phi(|e|) \leftarrow |e| + (k + 1)$;   `// Apply constant shift to the absolute error value`
7   **else**
8        $\phi(|e|) \leftarrow 2 * |e| + b$;   `// b ∈ {0, 1} is the next watermark bit to be embedded`
9    $\phi(e) \leftarrow sgn(e) * \phi(|e|)$;
10   **return** $\phi(e)$;

4.2.5 COMBINING MODIFIED ERRORS WITH PREDICTED PIXELS

Each predicted pixel, combined with its corresponding modified (watermark bit embedded) prediction error, produces a watermarked pixel. We combine a predicted pixel with a modified error using the following integer transformation:

$$p_{wm} = \xi(p) - \phi(e) = p + e - \phi(e), \tag{4.7}$$

where p_{wm} is the watermarked pixel.

Transformation (4.7) may produce some watermarked pixels falling outside the unsigned 8-bit integer range $[0, 255]$ causing an underflow ($p_{wm} < 0$) or an overflow ($p_{wm} > 255$). Handling of these situations will be presented in Section 4.3.1. Before that, we present our watermark extraction algorithm.

4.3 WATERMARK EXTRACTION ALGORITHM

Figure 4.3 presents a flowchart of the watermark extraction algorithm. For extraction, we select base pixels in the watermarked image, and predict the first, second and third sets of pixels subsequently, following the same procedure described in Sections 4.2.1–4.2.2. Locations of the base pixels and the three sets of predicted pixels are the same as shown in Fig. 4.1.

$$\phi(e) = \xi(p_{wm}) - p_{wm} \tag{4.8}$$

Next, forward transformation (4.8) is applied to each watermarked non-base pixel p_{wm} and its prediction $\xi(p_{wm})$, to compute the prediction error $\phi(e)$, from which the watermark bits are extracted.

Watermark bits are extracted from the prediction errors ($\phi(e)$), and the original errors (e) are restored, following Procedure 16. By the term *original errors* we refer to the prediction pixel errors, we achieved originally, before watermark embedding.

We apply the following transformation (4.9) (reverse of transformation (4.8)) to each $\{\xi(p_{wm}), e\}$ pair to restore the original cover image:

$$p = \xi(p_{wm}) - e. \tag{4.9}$$

Note that the values of $\xi(p)$ and $\xi(p_{wm})$ are equal since the base pixels are not modified during the process of embedding the watermark.

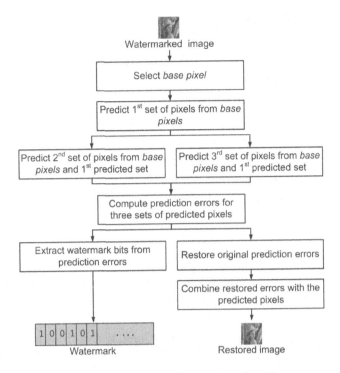

FIGURE 4.3: Watermark extraction algorithm.

Procedure 16: EXTRACT_WATERMARK

Input: Watermark bit embedded prediction error ($\phi(e)$), error threshold (k)

Output: Original prediction errors e

```
// Extract watermark bits and restore original prediction errors
```

1 **if** $\phi(e) < 0$ **then**

2     $sgn(e) \leftarrow -1$;

3 **else**

4     $sgn(e) \leftarrow +1$;

5 **if** $|\phi(e)| > (2 * k + 1)$ **then**

6     $|e| \leftarrow |\phi(e)| - (k + 1)$;

7 **else**

8     $b = mod(|\phi(e)|, 2)$;   // $b \in \{0, 1\}$ is the next watermark bit extracted

9     $|e| \leftarrow \frac{|\phi(e)| - b}{2}$;

10 $e \leftarrow sgn(\phi(e)) * |e|$;

11 **return** e;

4.3.1   HANDLING OF UNDER/OVERFLOW

If the application of transformation (4.7) to a particular $\{\xi(p), \phi(e)\}$ pair produces $p_{wm} \notin [0, 255]$, an *underflow* ($p_{wm} < 0$) or *overflow* ($p_{wm} > 255$) is said to have occurred. We simply do not embed into a prediction error ($\phi(e)$), which may cause such an under/overflow, and move on to the next.

While extracting, we test each prediction error to find out whether it can cause such under/overflow. To perform the test we first apply Procedure 15 to the prediction error with both $b = 0$ and $b = 1$, representing the watermark bits to be embedded; and then the transformation 4.7 is applied on the modified prediction error to produce the test watermarked pixel p_{wm}. This watermarked pixel is tested for under/overflow. A prediction error, found capable of causing under/overflow, during extraction, indicates one of the two possibilities.

1. It was found to be capable of causing under/overflow during embedding, and hence was not used for embedding.

2. Previously it was capable of undergoing embedding without causing an under/overflow, so was used for embedding, but after embedding it has lost its embedding capability.

For error-free extraction, we need to correctly infer, which of the above two possible cases has actually occurred. This differentiation is accomplished by the use of a binary bit string, termed as the *location map*. For each occurrence of the first case, we assign a "0" to the location map and for each occurrence of the second case we assign a "1" to the location map. If none of the above cases occurs, the location map is an empty bit string. During extraction, if an prediction error is found to be capable of causing under/overflow, we check the next location map bit. If we encounter a "0" in the location map, we do not use the corresponding prediction error for extraction and keep it unchanged. If we encounter a "1" in the location map, we apply Procedure 16 on corresponding prediction error to extract watermark bits and restore original prediction error.

4.4   OVERHEAD BITS

Apart from the watermark bits, some extra bits need to embedded into the cover image for correct working of our algorithm. Information represented by those *overhead bits* consist of two parts: (1) *location map* (number of overhead bits = length of location map) and (2) *error threshold k* (number of overhead bits = 8, since $0 \le k \le 255$).

The length of location map for our algorithm is extremely small, being zero for most of the test images we have considered. We can further reduce the number of overhead bits by losslessly compressing the location map, using *runlength encoding* or any other lossless compression algorithm, as well as assigning fewer than 8 bits for representing k which is generally chosen to be much smaller than 255. In our experiments (presented in Section 4.6) we varied the value of k within the range [0,10].

For insertion of the overhead bits we use the LSB positions of the base pixels beginning from the last base pixel. This insertion is done by replacing the LSBs of n_{ov} number of base pixel, where n_{ov} is the number of overhead bits. The end of n_{ov} bits is marked with a special end-of-message symbol. Before replacement, the original LSBs are collected into a bitstream which is concatenated at the beginning of the watermark. This resultant bitstream now acts as the payload and is embedded into the predicted pixels, more specifically, into their prediction errors. During extraction the overhead bits are collected from the LSB positions of the last n_{ov} base pixels and subsequently, LSBs of those base pixels are restored from the first n_{ov} payload bits extracted. Note that since LSB modification starts from the last base pixel, they do not affect the first n_{ov} predicted pixels, as a result the overhead bits are extracted without any error. This is possible because n_{ov} is extremely small in our scheme.

4.5   VARYING THE ERROR THRESHOLD

Depending on the size of the payload to be embedded, the need to embed greater number of bits into a cover image might arise. In such a scenario, the value of k can be increased, allowing errors with larger absolute values to be used for embedding, thus providing more space for embedding. With increase in the value of k, the amount by which the errors are modified ($\xi(|e|) \leftarrow |e| + (k+1)$) is also larger, increasing the distortion. But then, higher embedding capacity comes with higher cover-image distortion in all watermarking schemes. Hence, the *error threshold* parameter (k) provides us with a degree of freedom.

In the proposed scheme, a (sufficiently large) value of k is selected and the maximum embedding capacity it offers, limits the maximum size of payload that may be embedded. Otherwise, if the payload size is known a priori, k is to be varied to obtain sufficiently large embedding capacity. In this case, we may need to run the algorithm multiple times. However, the number of runs may be minimized by binary search or similar techniques.

4.6   EXPERIMENTAL RESULTS

The proposed algorithm was implemented in MATLAB. The performance of the algorithm was tested on six 512 × 512 pixels standard image processing test images shown in Fig. 4.4. The test images were chosen to have widely varying amounts of correlation among neighboring pixels, e.g., *Airplane*, has very high correlation, to *Mandrill* has very low correlation. Since reversible watermarking technique has major applications in security sensitive industries such as medical and military industries, we have also tested the performance of our algorithm on a range of medical images (shown in Figs. 4.5 and 4.6) as well as images used for military purposes (shown in Figs. 4.7 and

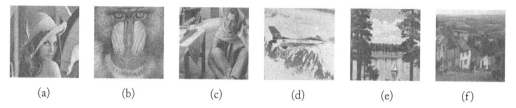

FIGURE 4.4: Standard image processing test images: (a) *Lena*; (b) *Mandrill*; (c) *Barbara*; (d) *Airplane*; (e) *Sailboat*; and (f) *Goldhill*.

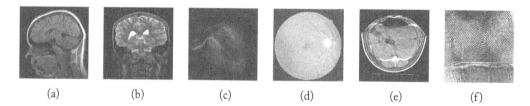

FIGURE 4.5: Biological test images: (a) *Algae*; (b) *Cellulas*; (c) *CRM1*; (d) *CRM2*; (e) *Chromo*; and (f) *Fluocel*.

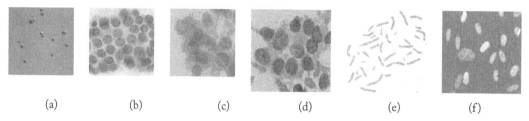

FIGURE 4.6: Medical test images: (a) *Brain*; (b) *Neck*; (c) *Heart*; (d) *Retina*; (e) *Xray*; and (f) *Fingerprint*.

4.8). All those images are standard medical and military test images. (Test image set credit: Model courtesy of Playboy Magazine, 1972 [50] and Computer Vision Group, University of Granada [51].)

The proposed reversible watermarking algorithm was tested to investigate its performance with respect to the following properties:

- maximum embedding capacity achievable; and

- distortion of watermarked image as compared to original cover image

Maximum embedding capacity of an image was evaluated by the number of pure watermark bits (not including the overhead bits) that can be embedded into the entire cover image as well as average number of bits that can be embedded per pixel, measured in units of bpp (*bits-per-pixel*). Distortion of the watermarked image was estimated in terms of *peak signal-to-noise ratio* (PSNR). To calculate

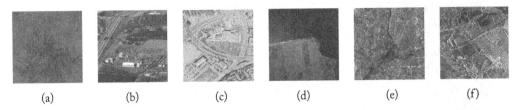

FIGURE 4.7: Aerial test images: (a) *Aerial 1*; (b) *Aerial 2*; (c) *Aerial 3*; (d) *Aerial 4*; (e) *Aerial 5*; and (f) *Aerial 6*.

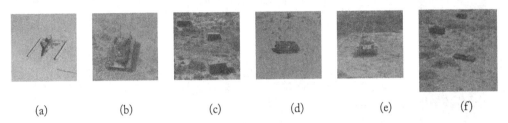

FIGURE 4.8: Military test images: (a) *Military 1*; (b) *Military 2*; (c) *Military 3*; (d) *Military 4*; (e) *Military 5*; and (f) *Military 6*.

the PSNR, first the mean square error (MSE) was calculated as:

$$MSE = \sum_{i=1}^{m} \sum_{j=1}^{n} \frac{\left(X_{org}(i,j) - X_{wm}(i,j)\right)^2}{m \cdot n},$$
(4.10)

where $X_{org}(i,j)$ is the (i,j)th pixel of the original image, $X_{wm}(i,j)$ is the (i,j)th pixel of the watermarked image, and m and n are the dimensions of the image (here each is 512). Then, PSNR was calculated as:

$$PSNR = 10 \log_{10} \left(\frac{MAX_I^2}{MSE}\right) \text{dB} = 10 \log_{10} \left(\frac{255^2}{MSE}\right) \text{dB},$$
(4.11)

where MAX_I is the maximum possible pixel value of the image, which is 255 in this case because of the 8–bit grayscale nature of the image.

In our experiments, the value of the *error threshold parameter* (k) was varied from 0–10. The effect of this variation on the embedding capacity (of the entire cover image) in bits is shown in Table 4.1 for our six 512×512 grayscale standard image processing test images. Table 4.1 also presents the watermarked image distortion results in terms of PSNR (in dB) for the six test images.

TABLE 4.1: Maximum embedding capacity and PSNR at different values of error threshold

Error Threshold (k)	Lena		Mandrill		Barbara		Airplane		Sailboat		Goldhill	
	Maximum Capacity (bits)	PSNR (dB)	Maximum Capacity (bits)	PSNR (dB)	Maximum Capacity (bits)	PSNR (dB)	Maximum Capacity (bits)	PSNR (dB)	Maximum Capacity (bits)	PSNR (dB)	Maximum Capacity (bits)	PSNR (dB)
0	46924	49.9728	9125	49.5170	18180	49.9711	36355	49.8372	16062	49.5986	16151	49.6289
1	103389	45.0614	26623	43.7303	51834	44.0814	90438	44.7445	45866	43.9964	46295	44.0009
2	131230	42.6762	42145	40.4826	78856	41.1261	122350	42.2479	69984	41.9656	72449	40.9917
3	147436	41.1448	55743	38.2538	98389	39.179	141551	40.682	89686	39.9477	94344	39.0157
4	157876	40.029	67294	36.5760	112385	37.7426	153438	39.5582	105918	37.4765	111995	37.5942
5	165008	39.175	77420	35.2424	122421	36.609	161188	38.6981	119495	36.3463	126333	36.518
6	170362	38.4849	86156	34.1408	130065	35.6732	166754	37.9934	130751	35.4473	138185	35.6729
7	174318	37.9123	94086	33.207	136025	34.8763	170840	37.4064	140158	34.7153	147616	34.9917
8	177445	37.4265	100995	32.4067	140959	34.1821	174101	36.8952	147916	34.1048	155063	34.4307
9	179978	37.0077	107049	31.7025	145134	33.5675	176714	36.4516	154409	33.5914	161297	33.9625
10	182038	36.6473	112710	31.0777	148687	33.0199	178867	36.0615	159880	33.1496	166312	33.5643

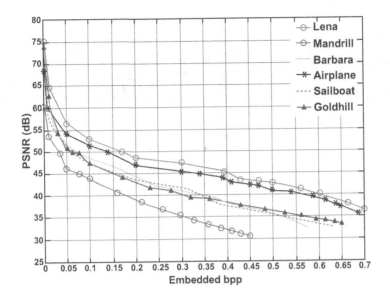

FIGURE 4.9: Plot of peak signal-to-Noise ratio (PSNR) vs. watermark bits embedded per pixel for standard image processing test images.

Results presented in Table 4.1 show that by increasing the value of k, a very high embedding capacity can be achieved at considerably low distortion.

Fig. 4.9 shows the variation of PSNR (in dB) with embedding capacity (in bpp), in bits-per-pixel, for all six test images. Note that the "embedding capacity" represents the number of pure watermark bits (not including overhead bits) embedded into the cover image.

4.6.1 APPLICATION TO MEDICAL AND MILITARY IMAGES

We have applied our algorithm to reversibly watermark a set of application-specific test images which include standard medical and military test images shown in Figs. 4.5–4.8. We have selected such a test set since medical and military industries are the primary application areas of reversible watermarking. The maximum embedding capacity and the corresponding watermarked cover-image distortion for all those images are presented in Table 4.2, where the value of the *error threshold* k was varied between 0 and 10. Figure 4.10 shows the variation of watermarked cover-image distortion (PSNR) with embedded bits-per-pixel for the medical and military test images considered, for $k \in [0, 10]$.

TABLE 4.2: Performance of proposed algorithm for 512 × 512 medical and military test images with $k \in [0, 10]$

Results for Biological Images			Results for Medical Images			Results for Aerial Images			Results for Military Images		
Image	Maximum Capacity (bits)	PSNR (dB)	Image	Maximum Capacity (bits)	PSNR (dB)	Image	Maximum Capacity (bits)	PSNR (dB)	Image	Maximum Capacity (bits)	PSNR (dB)
Algae	128361	33.5221	Brain	576224	39.8316	Aerial 1	77083	36.9379	Military 1	75534	45.3251
Cellulas	83667	30.9765	Neck	575636	38.8052	Aerial 2	101697	37.7925	Military 2	117800	46.2966
CRM1	585929	32.3301	Heart	86574	40.6316	Aerial 3	90636	37.0446	Military 3	99326	45.7221
CRM2	114202	32.1061	Retina	192889	40.4365	Aerial 4	67698	41.9861	Military 4	91307	45.6598
Chromo	155360	35.5092	Xray	142476	49.9275	Aerial 5	88839	35.4163	Military 5	103122	45.7066
Fluocel	52663	27.3101	Fingerprint	137553	31.6135	Aerial 6	68669	35.5666	Military 6	100455	45.7466

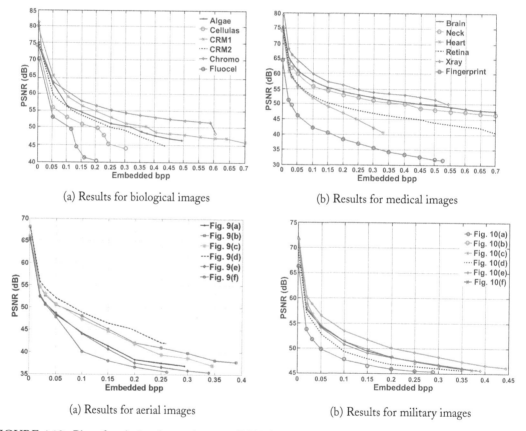

(a) Results for biological images

(b) Results for medical images

(a) Results for aerial images

(b) Results for military images

FIGURE 4.10: Plot of peak signal-to-noise ratio (PSNR) vs. watermark bits embedded per pixel. Results for (a) *Biological*; (b) *Medical*; (c) *Aerial*; and (d) *Military* images.

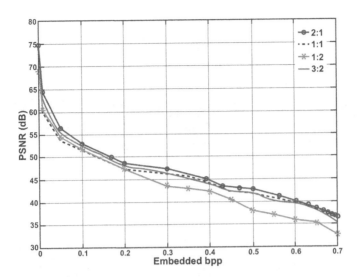

FIGURE 4.11: Comparison of Peak Signal-to-Noise Ratio (PSNR) vs. embedded bits-per-pixel plots for varying weights assigned to original and predicted neighbors. Test image used: 512 × 512 *Lena*.

4.6.2 VARYING THE WEIGHTS OF A WEIGHTED-MEDIAN FILTER

For computing the weighted-median of a set of pixels in our experiments, the weights assigned to the original and predicted pixels are in the ratio 2:1. Higher weights are assigned to the original pixels, as compared to the predicted pixels, to increase the accuracy of predicting, thus minimizing the absolute values of the prediction errors. Section 4.2.2 presents the details of pixel prediction in our algorithm.

In order to analyze the results of assigning different weights to the neighbors of a pixel while predicting its value, we varied the weights assigned to the original and the predicted neighbors. In all our experiments, we assigned weights to the original and the predicted neighbors in the ratio 2:1. In this section, we compared this result with those produced by using three other weight ratios. The weight ratios used here for the comparison are 2:1, 1:1, 1:2 and 3:2, where each represents the following ratio with respect to a particular pixel whose value is to be predicted:

weight assigned to an original neighboring pixel : weight assigned to a predicted neighboring pixel.

The comparison results are presented in Fig. 4.11 in form of cover-image distortion vs. number of embedded bpp for the *Lena* image.

4.7 SUMMARY

In this chapter we discussed, using an example, how a reversible watermarking algorithm works step-by-step. We discussed the working of a prediction-based reversible watermarking algorithm, since this class is one of the most widely ones in the current state-of-the-art. The algorithm works by exploiting the inherent spatial correlation among neighboring image pixels, where a pixel value is predicted from the weighted-median of its neighboring pixels. Assigned weights to the neighboring pixels help to make the predictions more accurate in this algorithm.

CHAPTER 5

Addressing Implementation Issues

Reversible watermarking algorithms, constituting a special subclass of digital watermarking (with the added advantage of distortion-free cover reversal) comes with a number of developmental and implementation challenges which are absent in their non-reversible counterparts. In this chapter, we discuss the major challenges involved in the design and implementation of reversible watermarking algorithms, along with possible solution approaches.

5.1 MANAGING AUXILIARY INFORMATION

To accomplish the reversibility property, additional retrieval information needs to be embedded into the cover image, in addition to the original watermark in reversible watermarking algorithms. In any general reversible watermarking, some regions (positions or pixel submatrices) of the cover image can embed higher number of payload bits than others. Retrieval information is used to differentiate regions (positions or pixel submatrices) of an image having watermark bits embedded, from those which could not embed any bit due to embedding capacity limitations. During watermark extraction and cover image retrieval, those pixels which have watermark bits embedded are used, and the rest are kept unmodified. However, in effect, embedding this additional retrieval information reduces the pure watermark embedding capacity. Thus, a major challenge for implementation of reversible watermarking algorithms is minimizing this retrieval information requirement, hence maximizing the pure watermark embedding capacity, while allowing complete distortion-free restoration of the cover image after watermark extraction.

Several techniques have been proposed to minimize the retrieval information requirement and embedding this retrieval information in addition to the watermark. An example of this additional information is the *location map* which is a binary bitstream used to distinguish between image positions having watermark bit(s) embedded and those having no watermark bit embedded. Location map is used widely in several state-of-the-art reversible watermarking algorithms such as *difference expansion* based algorithm of Tian [4], *quad-transform-based* algorithm of Weng et al. [11] or *integer DCT-based* algorithm of Yang et al. [6]. Other reversible watermarking algorithms also embed the cover image retrieval information into the watermarked image in some form or the other. For example, the interpolation based reversible watermarking algorithm proposed by Luo et al. [5]

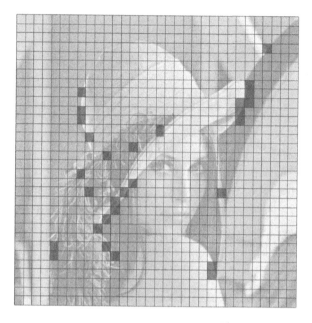

FIGURE 5.1: 512×512 *Lena* image divided into blocks for tamper localization in Tian's difference expansion based reversible watermarking algorithm [4].

embeds this information in the form of overhead bits into the marginal area of the watermarked image.

Our key observation in this respect is that for standard test images, the pixels incapable of accommodating watermark bits for any standard reversible watermarking algorithm are restricted to certain regions of the image, and these regions usually constitute only a small fraction of the area of the entire image. For example, Fig. 5.1 shows the scenario of applying Tian's difference expansion based reversible watermarking algorithm [4] to the 512×512 *Lena* image. In Fig. 5.1, the *Lena* image is divided into small regions of size 256 pixels each and the darker blocks represent those regions which contain at least one pixel incapable of accommodating any watermark bit. Hence, if we divide the cover image into small regions and embed the watermark as well as the retrieval information, corresponding to a region, into the region itself, the retrieval information requirement is hugely reduced. This is because, in the entire cover image, only those *few* regions covering the pixels incapable of embedding payload bits, are the regions which need retrieval information; other regions do not require any additional information. Therefore, region-wise retrieval information computation is a probable solution for minimizing retrieval information requirement, which may be explored by researchers in future.

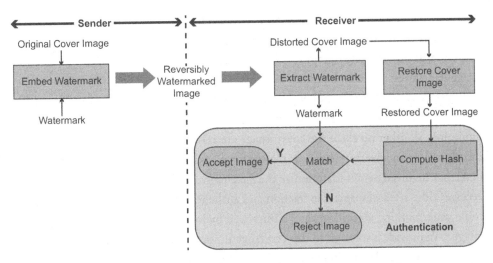

FIGURE 5.2: Authentication mechanism in reversible watermarking.

5.2   OPTIMIZING FALSE PIXEL REJECTION RATE

In reversible watermarking algorithms, the watermark is generally a secure hash of the cover image, which is generated by using any well-known cryptographic hash algorithm such as MD5 or SHA. At the receiver side, the watermark is extracted and the hash of the restored cover image is computed. The restored cover image is authenticated and accepted at the receiver end, only if the watermark and the computed hash match. A hash mismatch indicates that the image was tampered during transmission; consequently, the cover image is rejected at the receiver end due to authentication failure. The authentication mechanism in a generic reversible watermarking algorithm is depicted in Fig. 5.2. A hash mismatch may be brought about even by a single bit tampering in the cover image, causing the entire image to get rejected, pixel-by-pixel image recovery being the primary goal of reversible watermarking. Reversible watermarking being a *fragile watermarking* technique, such tampering is trivial for a "man-in-the-middle" adversary to perform.

Image tampering is not necessarily intentional always. Many times, reversibly watermarked image rejection at the receiver end due to a hash mismatch (and consequent authentication failure) is brought about by *unintentional modifications*. For example, during transmission through a noisy communication channel [63, 66], one or more pixels of an image may get modified. Such unintentional tampering of even a few pixels in a reversibly watermarked image causes the entire image to get rejected by the receiver; hence the need for subsequent retransmissions of the image arises. Examples of such unintentional tampering are often found in the military industry where the communication channels can be highly noisy [61, 64], an issue described in detail in Chapter 2. In such cases, although the cover image modification is unintentional in nature, it is bound to occur each time the image is transmitted. This causes the image to get rejected again and again even due to minimal modifications, in spite of repeated retransmissions of the entire image.

In general reversible watermarking algorithms, the convention is to reject the entire cover image at the receiver end if it fails authentication, even if it is due to minimal tampering of the cover image, since there is no way to detect the exact location(s) of tampering. Thus, even due to a single pixel tampering, all other pixels of the cover image are falsely rejected by the receiver. This feature may be exploited by an adversary to bring about a form of denial-of-service (DoS) attack. Hence, a major challenge involved here is to minimize the *False Rejection Rate* (FRR) of the cover image pixels at the receiver side, after watermark extraction and authentication procedures. The performance of a reversible watermarking algorithm can be improved by localizing the area(s) of tampering in the cover image. We provide a solution to this challenge in form of a tamper detection and localization approach, which we will discuss in details in the next chapter.

5.3   OPTIMIZING RUNTIME REQUIREMENTS

Due to complex mathematical operations involved in the implementation of reversible watermarking algorithms, such algorithms have considerably large runtime requirements compared to their non-reversible counterparts, and the reduction in such large runtime is one of the major challenges of design and implementation of reversible watermarking algorithms, especially in situations where real-time performance is a necessity. The complex, time-consuming mathematical operations involved in the algorithms include:

invertible functions such as invertible integer transform, invertible IDCT, etc.

computation of overhead data such as cover image retrieval information (location map), peak of pixel frequency histogram, thresholds, etc., and

lossless compression techniques [19] such as *JBIG*, *Run Length Encoding*, *LZW Encoding*, etc.

Many reversible watermarking algorithms, such as the IDCT-based algorithm of Yang et al. [6], have block-based implementation. The runtime requirements of such block-based reversible watermarking algorithms may always be improved by *parallelization* or *multi-threaded programming*. In addition, hardware accelerators, such as *Application Specific Integrated Circuit* (ASIC) and *Field Programmable Gate Array* (FPGA) based implementations are also promising in improving the processing-time of such algorithms.

5.4   DEVELOPMENT OF A COMMON EVALUATION PLATFORM

The present state-of-the-art evaluates and compares reversible watermarking algorithms with the help of extensive experimentation and simulation, in terms of traditional performance parameters: (1) watermark embedding capacity; (2) cover data distortion; and (3) distortion vs. capacity characteristics. However, current state-of-the-art lacks a common evaluation platform to compare and contrast multiple reversible watermarking schemes. In this chapter we present a software tool developed by us, for implementation and performance evaluation of state-of-the-art reversible watermarking algorithms.

The proposed application[1] is a MATLAB based software platform to evaluate several state-of-the-art reversible watermarking schemes for digital images (it also supports audio and video watermarking, but those features are outside the scope of the present work). The application comes with a Graphical User Interface (GUI) which provides push–button facilities for the user to pick and choose any number among an available selection of state-of-the-art digital reversible watermarking algorithms; select the cover image and watermark files, and then run the embedding and extraction algorithms. The embedding process produces detailed reports and comparison plots of "Pre-Extraction Peak Signal-to-Noise Ratio (PSNR)" (in dB) vs. "Embedding Capacity" (in bits-per-pixel or bpp) for all the algorithms for which the run was conducted. The application currently supports nine different state-of-the-art reversible watermarking algorithms for digital images, all of which are published in reputed peer–reviewed journals/conferences, and some of them we have developed and published ourselves. Additional codes for other state-of-the-art schemes can be easily plugged into the existing software in the future, as and when required.

The novel features of the application are:

1. a common platform capable of evaluating any state-of-the-art reversible watermarking algorithm, which was, until now, missing in the state-of-the-art;

2. presentation of evaluation parameters (embedding capacity in bpp and watermarked cover quality or PSNR in dB) with respect to varied algorithms as well as varied test (image and audio) data, on the fly while the algorithms are implemented;

3. presentation of watermarked cover quality vs. embedding capacity characteristics in the form of graphical plots for easy comparison of various schemes by the user;

---

1. Rajat Subhra Chakraborty, Ruchira Naskar, and Bittu Sarkar, "A Method and System for Evaluation of Reversible Watermarking of Digital Images and Audio," Indian patent filed in May 2013 (Ref: 853/KOL/2013).

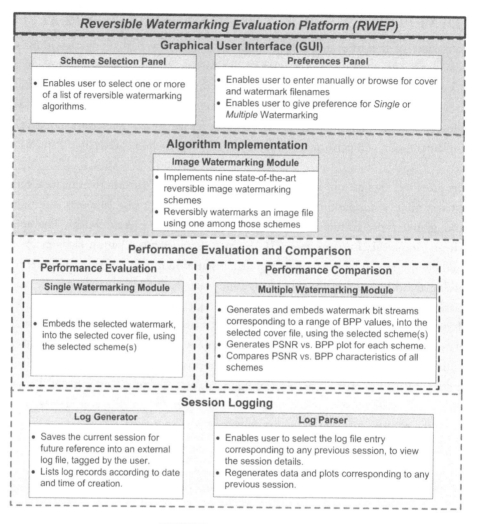

FIGURE 5.3: Block diagram.

4. real-time logging of the code execution process both in the MATLAB command window as well as in an external log file, for later reference of results obtained; and

5. finally, user ability to easily evaluate and compare existing state-of-the-art reversible image and audio watermarking schemes, using only a few push-button features provided by the invention.

Figure 5.3 illustrates a block representation of the system. It consists of four main components, discussed below:

1. a Graphical User Interface (GUI) and its software implementation;

2. implementation of the reversible watermarking algorithms supported (for both digital image and audio);

3. features of the GUI and their software implementation which allow a user to evaluate and compare the performance of the supported reversible watermarking algorithms (for both digital image and audio); and

4. features of the GUI and their software implementation which allow a user to save the current session, and retrieve it on demand at any later time.

5.4.1   WORKING METHODOLOGY

Figure 5.4 illustrates a operational flow-chart of the evaluation platform developed, the *reversible Watermarking Evaluation Platform (RWEP)*. There are two ways in which an image/audio can be watermarked using *RWEP*.

Method 1.   The cover file, the watermark file, and the watermarking algorithm(s) to run are selected from the *preference panel* by the user. The watermark used can be an image file or a bit stream written into a text file. This method produces one watermarked image/audio per watermarking algorithm selected.

Method 2.   In this case, multiple watermarks are selected per algorithm, in the form of bit streams, one differing from the other by its length in bits. These lengths are taken as input from the user as varying bpp values, with respect to a particular cover image/audio. At the end of this step, the watermarked data distortion (PSNR) vs. capacity (bpp) can be produced for individual image or audio, as well as a combined plot for the purpose of comparison.

A snapshot of the main application window is presented in Fig. 5.5. Note that the snapshot of Fig. 5.5 shows options for image, audio and video watermarking. However, since we are dealing only with digital image watermarking in this work, here we discuss only that part of the application (RWEP) which has been developed for reversible watermarking of digital images.

5.4.2   VIEWING PLOTS GENERATED IN THE PAST

The details of runtime sessions of the *RWEP* application are saved into an external *Log File* in form of time–stamped log records. The *RWEP* application provides option for the user to *tag* a particular session in the log file, during runtime. This feature is used for searching a particular session log, from a pool of available logs at a later point of time. Plots generated by the *RWEP* in the past can be regenerated by a subapplication called the *Log Parser*, by parsing the log file. Snapshot of the *Log Parser* window is shown in Fig. 5.6.

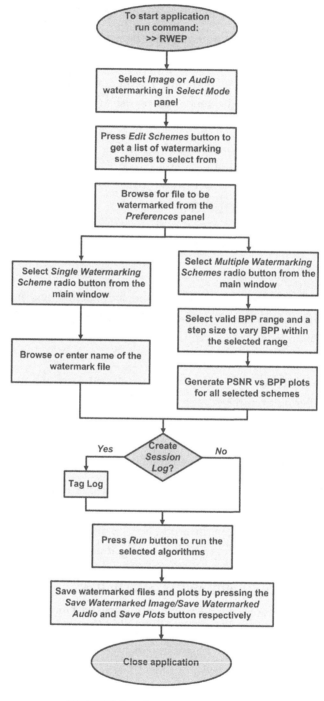

FIGURE 5.4: Operational flowchart.

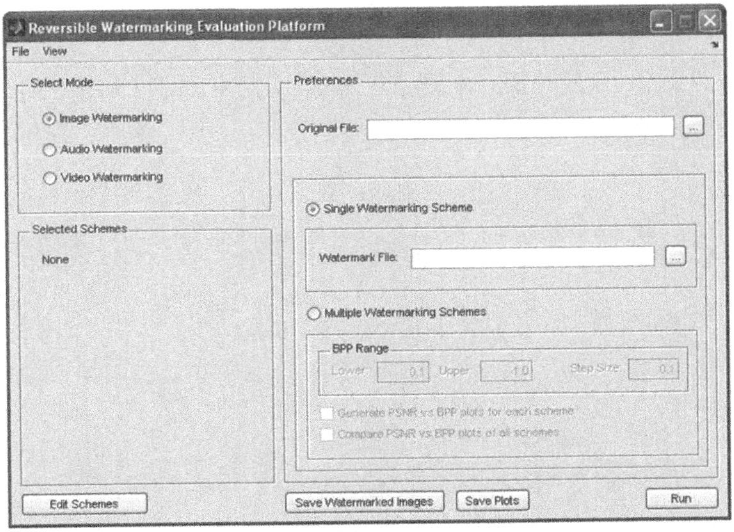

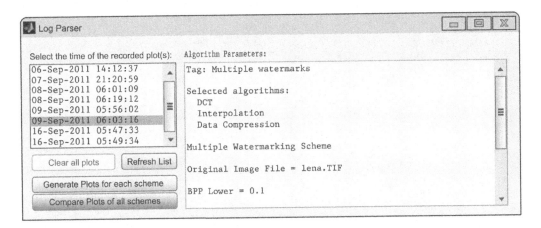

FIGURE 5.5: The *RWEP* application main window.

FIGURE 5.6: The *Log Parser* window.

5.5 SUMMARY

In this chapter we presented four major challenges behind the development and implementation of reversible watermarking algorithms. As a solution to one of the problems, we have presented *RWEP*, a software simulation based evaluation platform for testing the performance of reversible watermarking schemes and comparing them against each other (in terms of common performance metrics). Future research in this direction would also include development of a theoretic framework to analyze the performance of such algorithms saving the implementation cost.

CHAPTER 6

Reversible Watermarking with Tamper Localization Property

6.1 INTRODUCTION

In general reversible watermarking algorithms, the convention is to reject the entire cover image at the receiver end if it fails authentication, even if it is due to minimal tampering of the cover image, since there is no way to detect the exact location(s) of tampering. The performance of a reversible watermarking algorithm can be improved by localizing the area(s) of tampering in the cover image. In many practical cases of medical, legal or military image transmissions, which are the main application domains of reversible watermarking [4, 8], it is only some areas of the image, which carry the bulk of the important information, and is of interest to the recipient. In such cases it is beneficial for the receiving party to know whether the tampering has occurred within or outside their area of interest, since this knowledge helps to avoid unnecessary rejection of the entire cover image. We propose retransmission of only the tampered parts of the image, as a possible solution to minimize the *False Rejection Rate* (FRR) for cover image pixels and should completely suffice the user's requirements. In any reversible watermarking algorithm, the hash (watermark) is computed over the entire cover image. This hash facilitates the authentication of the entire cover image as a whole, but fails to authenticate the individual regions of the cover image at the receiver side. This causes rejection of the entire cover image in case of any tampering, even if the tampering is confined within a small part of the image. Hence in our solution, the entire image is divided into units of tamper localization and the hash of each individual unit is embedded into itself, in order to locate the tampered areas for the purpose of selective rejection. Such a tamper localization unit is also the unit of rejection in case of authentication failure.

In this section we discuss a generalized tamper localization approach for reversible watermarking algorithms. Unlike other state-of-the-art tamper localization approaches (such as [57, 70, 71, 72]), the proposed tamper localization approach [69] is a generalized one, that is applicable to any general reversible watermarking algorithm. For other state-of-the-art reversible watermarking algorithms having authentication or tamper localization property, these properties are algorithm specific.

This technique helps to solve two implementation challenges related to reversible watermarking algorithms, viz. minimizing false pixel rejection rate as well as managing auxiliary information, as discussed in Chapter 5.

In Section 6.2, we present the necessary background, followed by the theory behind development of this technique in Section 6.3. In Section 6.4, the actual tamper localization method will be described in detail, with the help of an example application. Our implementation and experimental results are presented in Section 6.5. The conclusions will be summarized in Section 6.6.

Next, we present a brief overview of previous related work and the general theory behind the proposed tamper localization technique.

6.2   NECESSARY BACKGROUND

The watermark in general reversible watermarking algorithms [4, 5, 6, 7, 14, 20] is a secure keyed hash of the cover image, which can be used to authenticate the restored cover image at the receiver side. In recent years a number of researchers have tried to bind authentication and tamper localization capabilities to watermarking schemes. In 2010, Tsai et al. [73] proposed a reversible visible watermarking with authentication, having additional protection features. The authors proposed the use of two secret keys: the first key is used to encrypt the hash value before embedding it into the cover image, while the second key is used to generate a random sequence of integers, which is added to the watermarked sub-image, to prevent unauthorized retrieval of an almost original cover image. In 2012, Wang et al. [74] proposed a reversible watermarking scheme for two-dimensional vector maps with authentication and tamper localization capabilities. In Wang et al.'s scheme, the unit of tamper localization is *map vertex/feature*. Localization accuracy is measured in terms of number of vertices/features detected as tampered. In 2009, Yan et al. [70] proposed an invisible reversible watermarking scheme for images, based on the principle of pixel difference histogram modification which is capable of detecting blockwise tampering in an image. Other invisible reversible image watermarking schemes, with tamper detection capabilities, were proposed by Wu [71], Lee et al. [57] and Bausys et al. [72] between 2006 and 2007. In this chapter, we compare the performance of our proposed scheme to the other state-of-the-art invisible reversible image watermarking schemes, having tamper detecting capabilities, in Section 6.5.

6.3   TAMPER LOCALIZATION IN REVERSIBLE WATERMARKING

In any reversible watermarking algorithm, the watermark embedded is generally a hash computed over the entire cover image. This hash facilitates the authentication of the entire cover image as a whole, but fails to authenticate the individual regions of the cover image at the receiver side. This causes rejection of the entire cover image in case of any tampering, even if the tampering is confined

Procedure 17: EMBED_LOCALIZED_HASH

1 Divide the cover image into tamper localization blocks;
2 **foreach** block B **do**
3   Compute $H \leftarrow$ Hash(B);
4   Embed H into B;

within a small part of the image. Our aim in this chapter is to enable selective rejection of the tampered regions of the image. In this section, we propose a generalized method which can detect and localize tampering in a reversibly watermarked image.

In order to locate tampered areas in a reversibly watermarked image for the purpose of selective rejection, we propose to divide the entire image into units of tamper localization and embed the hash of each individual unit into itself by Procedure 17 (***EMBED_LOCALIZED_HASH***). A block is the unit of tamper localization, thus also the unit of rejection in case of authentication failure. A block B is considered tampered if

$$1 \leq n_{tamper} \leq |B|, \tag{6.1}$$

where n_{tamper} is the number of pixels tampered in B and $|B|$ is the size of block B in pixels. The ideal situation is to divide the entire cover image into uniform blocks. At the same time, the blocks must be small enough to allow sufficient accuracy of tamper localization. The two desirable properties of a tamper localization scheme in reversible watermarking can be summarized as follows.

Resolution of Tamper localization. The smaller the tamper localization unit block size, the higher the accuracy of locating the position of tampering in a reversibly watermarked image.

Uniformity in Block Sizes. Equal-sized tamper localization blocks over all areas of the cover image, to be reversibly watermarked.

The uniformity in tamper localization block sizes can be maintained only if it is possible to embed an equal number of hash bits in each block. In any general reversible watermarking algorithm some regions (positions or pixel submatrices) of the cover image can embed a higher number of payload bits than others, and this is the only reason of using additional retrieval information called the *location map* in such algorithms [4, 6, 11]. Location map is a binary bitstream used to differentiate regions (positions or pixel submatrices) of an image having watermark bits embedded, from those that could not embed any bit due to embedding capacity limitations, with the primary requirement of any reversible watermarking algorithm being restoration of the cover image back to its original form, additional retrieval information is embedded into the cover image in addition to the original watermark, to accomplish this reversibility. Location map is nothing but an example of such additional retrieval information required in reversible watermarking algorithms. Location map is used widely in several state-of-the-art reversible watermarking algorithms such as *difference expansion* based algorithm of Tian [4], *quad-transform-based* algorithm of Weng et al. [11] or *integer DCT* based algorithm of Yang et al. [6]. Other reversible watermarking algorithms also embed the cover image retrieval information into the watermarked image in some form or the other. For example, the recent interpolation based reversible watermarking algorithm proposed by Luo et al. [5] embeds this information in the form of overhead bits, into the marginal area of the watermarked image.

In summary, for reversible watermarking algorithms, the embedding capacity, and hence the cover image retrieval information requirement, varies from region to region of an image. This variation hinders the division of a cover image into uniform tamper localization blocks, since all blocks may not be equally capable of accommodating its share of hash bits. However, we provide a solution to this problem in form of a Block Merging Technique described later in Section 6.4.1.

6.3.1 BOUND ON TAMPER LOCALIZATION BLOCK SIZE

The above discussion makes it clear that to allow distortion-free recovery of the entire cover image, apart from the hash of a particular block we also need to embed the retrieval information corresponding to the block into itself. That is,

$$\text{Watermarked Block} \leftarrow \text{Original Block} \cup \text{Block Hash} \cup \text{Block Retrieval Information.} \quad (6.2)$$

For tamper localization in reversible watermarking, the first parameter to estimate before watermarking an image is the size of tamper localization blocks into which the image is to be divided uniformly. In this book, we obtained a bound on the tamper localization block size for a particular reversible watermarking algorithm and a particular image by the following way. Let the cover image (to be watermarked) be $\mathcal{I}$ containing $n \times m$ pixels and the reversible watermarking algorithm selected be $\mathcal{A}$. First, we obtain the maximum watermark embedding capacity of $\mathcal{I}$. Let the maximum number of pure watermark bits that can be embedded into $\mathcal{I}$ by $\mathcal{A}$ be b. Next, we find out the retrieval information requirement of $\mathcal{I}$. Let $\mathcal{I}$ require $|\delta|$ bits for cover image retrieval. Since in any general reversible watermarking algorithm, the retrieval information is also embedded into the cover image in addition to the pure watermark, the total payload embedding capacity of $\mathcal{A}$ is $b + |\delta|$ bits. Here the payload includes both the watermark as well as cover image retrieval information. Thus, each pixel of $\mathcal{I}$ can embed $\frac{b+|\delta|}{n \times m}$ payload bits on an average. Let the chosen hash algorithm return a hash bitstring consisting of $|H|$ bits. It follows from the above discussion that $|H|$ hash bits require at least $\frac{|H|}{(b+|\delta|)/(n \times m)}$ pixels to be embedded. Thus, the minimum tamper localization block size for

$\mathcal{A}$, when applied to $\mathcal{I}$ is given by:

$$|B| \geq \frac{|H| \times n \times m}{b + |\delta|}, \qquad (6.3)$$

where $|B|$ is the size of a unit tamper localization block in pixels and m, n are the dimensions of the cover image. $|H|$, b and $|\delta|$ are the hash bitstring length, maximum size of watermark that can be embedded, and space requirement for cover image retrieval information requirement, respectively, each in bits.

Since the experimental results to be presented next are for standard (benchmark) digital images, which are generally square or rectangular in dimension, we propose to select the tamper localization unit blocks as square or rectangular pixel submatrices, each consisting of $|B|$ pixels. The only condition is that, the division of an image into unit tamper localization blocks should be *uniform* and *complete*. That is, all unit tamper localization blocks should be of the same size and must completely cover the entire image.

6.4   THE METHOD OF TAMPER LOCALIZATION

We now describe a method to detect and localize tampering in a reversibly watermarked image. This method is a general one and is applicable to all reversible watermarking algorithms, which follow the basic operating principle of Fig. 5.2. As we have previously discussed, reversible watermarking algorithms need to embed retrieval information into the cover image, in addition to the watermark or the hash, for distortion-free restoration of the cover image after watermark extraction. This retrieval information is needed because every pixel of an image is not capable of embedding payload bits equally, with respect to a particular reversible watermarking algorithm. The retrieval information allows us to distinguish between the pixels having watermark bit(s) embedded and those which do not have any bit embedded.

Our key observation in this book is that for standard test images, the pixels incapable of accommodating payload bits for any standard reversible watermarking algorithm are restricted to certain regions of the image. In the proposed method we divide the cover image into blocks and embed the hash bits as well as the retrieval information, corresponding to a block, into the block itself. Now since only certain regions of the image contain pixels incapable of embedding payload bits, the blocks covering those regions are the only blocks in the entire image which need additional retrieval information; the blocks falling outside those regions do not require any retrieval information.

6.4.1   MERGING OF TAMPER LOCALIZATION UNIT BLOCKS

By the proposed method, we embed retrieval information *only* into those blocks of the cover image which require so, for error-free watermark extraction and cover image restoration. As a result, the

---

Procedure 18: BLOCK_MERGING

1 Divide the cover image into tamper localization unit blocks;   // Each consisting of $|B|$ pixels,
                                                                        // where $|B|$ is obtained by Eq. 6.3

2 **foreach** block B **do**

3   Set $flag(B) = 0$;   // B has not yet been merged with any other block

4 **foreach** block B **do**

5   Compute $H \leftarrow$ Hash(B);

6   **if** $flag(B) = 0$ **then**

7   **if** effective embedding capacity of B is less than $|H|$ **then**

8   Merge B with any three of its *unmerged adjacent unit* neighbors N_1, N_2, N_3
                 to form a merged block;

9   Set $flag(B) = flag(N_1) = flag(N_2) = flag(N_3) = 1$;   // All these four blocks
                                                                             // are merged together

---

pure hash embedding capacities of those blocks reduce, and often this effective embedding capacity falls below the actual size of the hash. So we merge such a block with its adjacent blocks to form a larger block, with an effective embedding capacity at least as high as what is required to embed the entire hash bitstream. In addition, we also found that for standard test images, the number of blocks merged by this procedure is optimal, since the blocks needed to be merged together due to low effective embedding capacity are located in close vicinity of each other. In many cases, due to high spatial correlation of pixel values, such blocks are situated adjacent to each other in an image. This property has allowed us to obtain optimum accuracy of tamper localization by the proposed method. For example, Fig. 6.1 shows the blocks of the *Lena* image which need retrieval information (panel (a)), and the merged blocks (panel (b)), while application of the proposed method to Hu et al.'s [7] reversible watermarking algorithm. The subfigure on the left shows that the blocks requiring retrieval information are positioned adjacent to each other in the image.

In Procedure 18 (**BLOCK_MERGE**), we present the proposed block merging technique in form of an algorithm. Procedure 18 first divides the entire cover image uniformly into unit blocks of size $|B|$ pixels, where $|B|$ is chosen as the minimum integer satisfying Eq. (6.3) (step 1). Initially, we mark each unit block B as unmerged in steps 2–3. Next, we traverse the entire cover image block by block, sequentially. Whenever we encounter the next unmerged unit block, with effective watermark embedding capacity less than the hash size, we merge it with three of its *unmerged adjacent unit* neighbors N_1, N_2, N_3 to form one merged block (steps 6–8). That is, four $x \times y$ unit blocks are merged into one $2x \times 2y$ merged block. Finally, we mark the four blocks B, N_1, N_2, N_3 as merged in step 9. In our work, we merged four adjacent unit blocks to form one merged block as this has

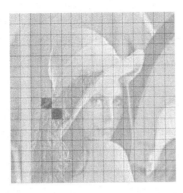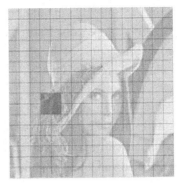

FIGURE 6.1: Tamper localization in Hu et al.'s reversible watermarking: (a) 512×512 *Lena* cover image divided into tamper localization blocks of size 32×32 pixels. Overflow blocks shown in darker shade. (b) Merged block of size 64×64 pixels, shown in darker shade.

provided an embedding capacity high enough to embed the 128-bit hash used in our experiments for our entire test set. For higher embedding capacity requirements, higher number of unit blocks may be merged together or unit blocks of larger size (as determined by Eq.(6.3)) should be used.

Next, we will present an example application of the proposed tamper localization method to Hu et al.'s [7] difference expansion based reversible watermarking algorithm with improved overflow location map.

6.4.2 AN APPLICATION

In this section, we present an application of the above tamper localization method. The test image used is the standard grayscale 512×512 *Lena* image. The hash algorithm considered for our experiments is standard 128-bit MD5 [75] which produces a 128-bit hash-based message authentication code (MAC). The MD5 algorithm has been used for (1) its enhanced security feature due to its keyed nature and preimage resistance, and (2) to obtain collision resistance, hence low false block rejection rate during tamper localization. We also considered using 8-bit or 16-bit Cyclic Redundancy Check (CRC) [65, 76], codes instead of 128-bit MD5 hash, to reduce the tamper localization block size. The above properties are absent in error detecting codes such as CRC. Although using shorter error detecting codes instead of cryptographic hash function, will lower the tamper localization block size; this will severely reduce the security and tampered block identification accuracy, due to absence of the above mentioned properties. However, in the case of reduced block size being the more desirable property, shorter error detecting codes such as CRC can always be used in our scheme instead of cryptographic hash, but at the cost of compromising the security and accuracy of the scheme.

With the use of 128-bit MD5 in our example, the minimum tamper localization unit block size for the *Lena* image was computed as 1024 pixels, by Eq. (6.3). Before going into further details on tamper localization, we briefly present the operating principle of Hu et al.'s reversible watermarking scheme, details of which can be found in [7].

Hu et al.'s Reversible Watermarking

The operation of Hu et al.'s [7] reversible watermarking algorithm is based on the principle of "prediction error histogram shifting." In Hu et al.'s scheme, a pixel x of the cover image is predicted as $\hat{x}$ from its right, diagonal and lower neighbors, a, b and c, respectively, by the following formula:

$$\hat{x} = \begin{cases} \max(a, c) & \text{if } b \leq \min(a, c) \\ \min(a, c) & \text{if } b \geq \max(a, c) \\ a + c - b & \text{otherwise.} \end{cases} \tag{6.4}$$

A prediction error e is computed as $e = x - \hat{x}$. The prediction error frequency histogram is formed. In standard test images, most of the prediction errors are concentrated towards zero. Next, two thresholds T_r and T_l are assumed, which divide the prediction error histogram into two parts: inner region for watermark embedding and outer region for error shifting in order to avoid pixel value overlap. The inner region is represented by $[-T_l, T_r - 1]$. The left and right outer regions are $[-e_l, -T_l - 1]$ and $[T_r, e_r]$, respectively, where $-e_l$ and e_r are the minimum and maximum error values.

Watermark embedding in the inner region of the histogram is done by following two steps. First, embedding the next watermark bit $b \in [0, 1]$, into the error e by: $e' = 2 \times e + b$. Second, adding the modified error e' to the predicted pixel $\hat{x}$ by: $x' = \hat{x} + e'$. Due to the watermark embedding procedure, some errors are moved out of the inner region to the outer regions. This may cause overlap of error values in the outer regions. To avoid any possible overlap, the error values in the outer regions are shifted outward a priori, in the following way. If an error e belongs to the left outer region, shift it as $e' = e - T_l$. If e belongs to the right outer region, shift it as $e' = e + T_r$. Finally, add the shifted error e' to the predicted pixel $\hat{x}$: $x' = \hat{x} + e'$.

Now some pixels of the cover image (considering it as an 8-bit image) may not be suitable for embedding or shifting, since in those cases the resultant x' is not a valid pixel value, i.e., $x' \notin [0, 255]$. Those pixels are said to cause overflow, and are simply ignored or kept unmodified during the embedding/shifting step. In order to facilitate reversibility during extraction, there must be a way to differentiate such pixels from those which were modified by embedding/shifting. This is done by the use of a binary bitstream called *overflow location map* or simply location map. The location map stores a "1" corresponding to a pixel capable of causing overflow, and a "0" for a pixel which can successfully embed/shift. The extraction procedure is straightforward and is done in just the reverse way of the embedding procedure. For reversible extraction, the location map is checked. If the next location map bit is "1", the pixel is kept unmodified. If it is "0", the pixel value is shifted towards zero or watermark bit extracted from the pixel, depending on whether the prediction error belongs to the outer or inner histogram region, respectively.

Watermark Embedding

For tamper localization in our test 512×512 *Lena* image, we first divided the entire image into unit blocks of size $32 \times 32 = 1024$ pixels (according to results obtained by Eq. (6.3)), as shown in Fig. 6.1(a). Next, we apply Hu et al.'s scheme on the individual unit blocks, to find out which of them have an embedding capacity less than the hash size or may cause overflow, hence need to store additional retrieval information. A block is called an *overflow block*, if at least one of its constituent pixels is capable of causing overflow after embedding/shifting by Hu et al.'s scheme. The overflow blocks of the test *Lena* image are shown in a darker shade, in Fig. 6.1(a). Note that due to minimized location map size in Hu et al.'s reversible watermarking algorithm, the number of overflow blocks in an image is very low; in our example, we have only two overflow blocks in the *Lena* image. As is evident from Fig. 6.1(a), the overflow blocks are located in close vicinity of each other with respect to the entire cover image, which is generally the case for any standard test image, due high spatial correlation among pixels.

Since an overflow block needs to store additional retrieval information, its pure hash embedding capacity may fall below the actual hash size, here 128 bits. According to Section 6.4.1, an overflow block is merged with its adjacent unit blocks in order to produce sufficient effective hash embedding capacity. The merged block of size 64×64 pixels in our test *Lena* image is shown in Fig. 6.1(b). Note that in this example application, since the two overflow unit blocks are located close to each other, they could be merged together into a single block. Now the merged larger block has a higher embedding capacity, and thus can embed its hash as well as whatever additional information is required for its retrieval. The only issue here is to correctly differentiate between the unit blocks and the merged blocks during extraction. We solve this simply by replacing the least significant bit (LSB) of the first pixel (pixel at position (1,1)), in each block, by an *block identification bit*. Before this replacement, the original first pixel LSB of each block is saved by appending it to the hash bit-stream, so the LSB can be correctly restored during cover image retrieval. During extraction, if LSB of the first pixel of a block is "0", it implies that the block has not been merged and does not carry any location map information. If LSB of the first pixel of a block is "1", it implies that the block has been merged with its neighboring blocks and the merged block carries location map information in addition to the hash, which would be needed for its exact recovery.

Finally, the payload to be embedded into each block is generated. For a unit block (block that is not merged), the payload comprises of nothing but its hash bitstream appended with the original LSB of the first block pixel. In case of a merged block, in addition to the hash and the *block identification bit*, the location map also needs to be stored within the block itself. To reduce the storage space requirement, we have losslessly compressed the location map (of individual merged blocks) by Run Length Encoding (RLE) [19], in our experiments. We find out the maximum possible compressed location map size for any merged block in a cover image, and represent it by $n_{loc\_map\_max}$. It was observed from our experiments that for a 64×64 merged block, the compressed location map size never exceeds 127 bits; hence we set $n_{loc\_map\_max}$ = 127 here. For a merged block, the bitstream X is obtained by concatenating the compressed location map to the *block identification bit* ("1").

$$X \leftarrow \text{block identification bit ("1") || compressed location map.} \tag{6.5}$$

According to our experimental results, the maximum length of X is $n_{loc\_map\_max} + 1 = 128$ bits for a 64×64 merged block. Now, the LSBs of the first 128 pixels (pixels at positions (1,1) through (2,64), constituting the first two rows) of a 64×64 merged block are replaced by the bits of X. Before this replacement, the original LSBs of the first ($n_{loc\_map\_max} + 1$) pixels of each merged block are saved by appending them to the hash bitstream, so that they can be placed back to their original positions during cover image retrieval. Thus, for a merged block, the payload comprises of its hash bitstream appended with the original LSBs of the first ($n_{loc\_map\_max} + 1$) block pixels.

The payload corresponding to each block is embedded into itself by Hu et al.'s reversible watermark embedding algorithm. In a unit block, the first pixel of the block is ignored during payload embedding, since it carries the *block identification bit*. Similarly in a merged block, no embedding/shifting operation is performed on the first ($n_{loc\_map\_max} + 1$) pixels, since they carry the *block identification bit* and the compressed location map. The reversible watermark embedding algorithm is shown in Procedure 19 (**EMBED**).

Watermark Extraction and Authentication

Procedure 20 (**EXTRACT & AUTHENTICATE**) presents the watermark extraction algorithm. During extraction, the watermarked image is first divided into tamper localization unit blocks, each consisting of 32×32 pixels. We extract the *block identification bit* from the first pixel's LSB position of each block. If it is "0", the block is identified as a unit block (not having been merged with any other block) and its payload is extracted by Hu et al.'s scheme, ignoring the first pixel. From the extracted payload, the block hash and original first pixel LSB are separated. The entire block, including the first pixel LSB, is restored back to its original form. Extraction procedure for a unit tamper localization block is shown in steps 8–12 of Procedure 20.

The *block identification bit* being "1" indicates that the current unit block belongs to a larger merged block. In a merged block, the compressed location map is extracted from the LSBs of its first $n_{loc\_map\_max} + 1 = 128$ pixels. It is then losslessly decompressed to obtain the original block

Procedure 19: EMBED

1 Divide the cover image into tamper localization blocks;

2 **foreach** block B **do**

3   Compute $H \leftarrow$ Hash(B);

4   **if** B is a 32×32 unit block **then**

5   Generate payload $P \leftarrow H \parallel \text{LSB}(B(1,1))$;   // $B(i, j)$ represents the (i, j)th pixel of B

6   Replace $\text{LSB}(B(1,1)) \leftarrow$ block identification bit $'0'$;

7   Embed P into pixels $[B(1,2)..B(32,32)]$;

8   **else if** B is a 64×64 merged block **then**

9   Compute $\delta \leftarrow$ Retrieval Information (location map) for B;

10   Generate $\delta_c \leftarrow$ Losslessly compressed δ;   // Run Length Encoding used here

11   Generate $X \leftarrow$ block identification bit $'1' \parallel \delta_c$;

12   Generate payload $P \leftarrow H \parallel \text{LSB}([B(1,1)...B(2,64)])$; // Since $(n_{loc\_map\_max} + 1) = 128$ here,
                                                              // LSBs of first two pixel rows of B are saved

13   Replace $\text{LSB}([B(1,1)..B(2,64)]) \leftarrow X$;

14   Embed P into pixels $[B(3,1)..B(64,64)]$;

retrieval information, using which the payload is extracted and the block restored back to its original form by Hu et al.'s scheme, ignoring its first two pixel rows. The hash and the original LSBs of the first 128 pixels of the merged block are separated from the payload. Extraction procedure for a merged tamper localization block is shown in steps 13–22 of Procedure 20.

Finally, the hash of each unit or merged block is computed, and matched with the corresponding extracted hash for tamper localization. Hash mismatch for any block implies that the block is tampered. The blocks failing authentication are rejected by the receiver.

In our extraction algorithm of Procedure 20, each merged block is accessed and processed only once. This achieved by the use of a $flag$ variable corresponding to each unit block. All flags are initially reset to zero (steps 2–3). Once a unit block is accessed for the first time, its $flag$ is set at step 6. Note that step 6 is executed for one and only one constituent (unit block) member of a merged block, which is essentially the first member that we encounter while scanning the image. For all other members the $flag$ variables are set by steps 20–21 after they are processed. Thus, the $flag$ variable corresponding to a particular unit block, when set to one, implies either one of the following two situations.

1. The present unit block is an unmerged block, and it has been processed by steps 9–12.

2. The present unit block belongs to a merged block which has been processed by steps 14–22.

Procedure 20: EXTRACT & AUTHENTICATE

1 Divide the cover image into tamper localization unit blocks of size 32×32 pixels
2 **foreach** unit block B **do**
3   Set $flag(B) \leftarrow 0$;   // $flag$ variable used to mark an already accessed unit block
4 **foreach** unit block B **do**
5   **if** $flag(B) == 0$ **then**   // unit block B has not yet been accessed
6   Set $flag(B) \leftarrow 1$;   // mark B as accessed
7          $block\_identification\_bit \leftarrow \text{LSB}(B(1,1))$;
8   **if** $block\_identification\_bit ==' 0'$ **then**   // B was not merged
9   Extract payload P from pixels $[B(1,2)..B(32,32)]$;
10   Restore pixels $[B(1,2)..B(32,32)]$;   // no retrieval information needed here
11   Separate hash $H \leftarrow$ first 128 payload bits $P(1:128)$;
12   Restore $\text{LSB}(B(1,1)) \leftarrow$ last payload bit $P(129)$;
13   **else if** $block\_identification\_bit ==' 1'$ **then**   // B is part of 64×64 merged block B_{merged}
14   Extract compressed location map $\delta_c \leftarrow \text{LSB}([B_{merged}(1,2)..B_{merged}(2,64)])$;
15   Generate location map $\delta \leftarrow$ Losslessly decompressed δ_c; // Run Length Decoding used here
16   Extract payload P from pixels $[B_{merged}(3,1)..B_{merged}(64,64)]$ using δ;
17   Restore pixels $[B_{merged}(3,1)..B_{merged}(64,64)]$ using δ;
18   Separate hash $H \leftarrow$ first 128 payload bits $P(1:128)$;
19   Restore $\text{LSB}([B_{merged}(1,1)..B_{merged}(2,64)]) \leftarrow$ last 128 payload bits $P(129:256)$;
20   **foreach** unit block N forming B_{merged} **do**
21   Set $flag(N) \leftarrow 1$;   // mark each merged neighbor of B as accessed
22   Set $B \leftarrow B_{merged}$;
23   **if** $H \mathrel{!=} \text{Hash}(B)$ **then**
24   Reject B;   // infer B as tampered

Once the $flag$ corresponding to a particular block B is set to one, it implies that the watermark extraction as well as block recovery procedures are over for B, and thus B is never again processed by steps 6–24.

Similar to the example application presented in this chapter, our proposed method of tamper localization can be applied to any general reversible watermarking algorithm, with slight modification in implementation parameters, the basic principle of operation remaining the same. In this chapter, we have applied the proposed method of tamper localization to five different state-of-the-art reversible watermarking algorithms, apart from Hu et al.'s algorithm. The experimental results and discussions pertaining to those are presented in Section 6.5.

6.4.3   FALSE REJECTION AS A CONSEQUENCE OF BLOCK MERGING

We proposed selective rejection of tampered blocks, in order to reduce the rate of cover image rejection in case of authentication failure. As stated previously in Section 6.3, the unit tamper localization blocks are the units of tamper localization, as well as rejection in an cover image by the proposed method. The ideal scenario to achieve 0% false rejection rate by the proposed method is the rejection of *only* those unit blocks which fail authentication at the receiver end. But in practical situations, this condition can not always be satisfied due to the *block merging feature* of the proposed scheme. When a group of tamper localization unit blocks are merged together for obtaining higher effective hash embedding capacity, the expanded block acts as the unit of rejection. Consequently, even for a single tampered unit block within the merged group of blocks, the entire group is rejected. In other words, except the actually tampered blocks(s), all other members of the group are *falsely rejected*. This increases the false rejection rate of the proposed method above 0%, for images having one or more merged blocks with tampering. However, for tampering detected in any unmerged unit tamper localization block, there is no false rejection of tamper localization blocks. Also, it was observed through our experiments that by the proposed method, the percentage of merged blocks is very low compared to that of the unmerged unit blocks for standard test images. As a result, the overall false rejection rate of tamper localization blocks produced by the proposed method is considerably low, as is evident from our experimental results also. The robustness of the proposed method against false rejection will be investigated further in Section 6.5.1.

6.5   EXPERIMENTAL RESULTS AND DISCUSSION

The proposed tamper localization method for reversible watermarking was implemented in MAT-LAB and tested on a set of test images. In this chapter we present our experimental results for the 8-bit, 512×512 test images shown in Fig. 6.2. Our test images included standard image processing test images as well as medical and military images, to make our test cases representative of the domains of application of reversible watermarking.

We now present the results of tamper localization by the proposed method, when applied on the following state-of-the-art reversible watermarking algorithms, each belonging to a specific class according to Feng et al.'s [8] classification:

- Hu et al.'s algorithm based on the principle of Difference Expansion [7];

- Tian's algorithm based on the principle of Difference Expansion [4];

- Celik et al.'s algorithm based on the principle of Data Compression [14];

- Ni et al.'s algorithm based on the principle of Histogram Bin Shifting [20];

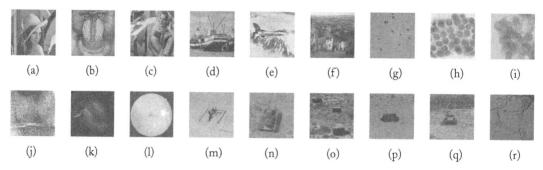

FIGURE 6.2: Our 512 × 512 test images. Standard image processing test images: (a) *Lena*; (b) *Mandrill*; (c) *Barbara*; (d) *Barche*; (e) *Plane*; and (f) *Goldhill*. Medical test images: (g) *Medical_img 1*—(l) *Medical_img 6*. Military test images: (m) *Military_img 1*—(r) *Military_img 6*.

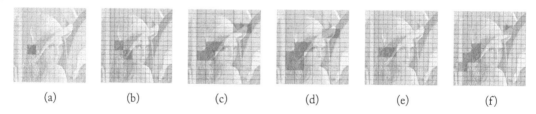

FIGURE 6.3: Merged blocks of the 512 × 512 *Lena* image, shown in darker shade. Reversible watermarking algorithm used: (a) Hu et al.'s algorithm [7]; (b) Tian's algorithm [4]; (c) Celik et al.'s algorithm [14]; (d) Ni et al.'s algorithm [20]; (e) Luo et al.'s algorithm [5]; and (f) Yang et al.'s algorithm [6].

- Luo et al.'s algorithm based on the principle of Pixel Prediction [5]; and

- Yang et al.'s algorithm based on the principle of Integer DCT [6].

In our implementation of the proposed scheme, we have used a 128-bit Message Authentication Code generated using the MD5 cryptographic hash function [75], to hash the tamper localization blocks. Figure 6.3 shows the tamper localization blocks of the 512 × 512 *Lena* image, for tamper localization using the above-mentioned reversible watermarking algorithms. The size of a tamper localization unit block, for the same image, varies according to the embedding capacity of the algorithm, which is evident from Eq. (6.3), as $|B| \propto \frac{1}{b}$. For all the test images of Fig. 6.2, the number and size of unit blocks (determined by Eq. (6.3)) as well as the number and size of merged blocks are presented in Table 6.1. It is evident from our experimental results in Table 6.1, that for most of the test images, the number of merged blocks is close to zero. This proves that in most standard test images, only a few blocks need retrieval information due to high spatial correlation of pixels in standard images.

TABLE 6.1: Tamper localization block requirements for different test images

Hu et al.'s algorithm

Image	No. of 32 × 32 Unit Blocks	No. of 64 × 64 Merged Blocks	Image	No. of 32 × 32 Unit Blocks	No. of 64 × 64 Merged Blocks	Image	No. of 32 × 32 Unit Blocks	No. of 64 × 64 Merged Blocks
Lena	252	1	Medical_img 1	256	0	Military_img 1	256	0
Mandrill	220	9	Medical_img 2	256	0	Military_img 2	256	0
Barbara	196	15	Medical_img 3	256	0	Military_img 3	252	1
Barche	256	0	Medical_img 4	244	3	Military_img 4	248	2
Plane	256	0	Medical_img 5	256	0	Military_img 5	256	0
Goldhill	256	0	Medical_img 6	244	3	Military_img 6	248	2

Tian's algorithm

Image	No. of 32 × 32 Unit Blocks	No. of 64 × 64 Merged Blocks	Image	No. of 32 × 32 Unit Blocks	No. of 64 × 64 Merged Blocks	Image	No. of 32 × 32 Unit Blocks	No. of 64 × 64 Merged Blocks
Lena	248	2	Medical_img 1	252	1	Military_img 1	240	4
Mandrill	140	14	Medical_img 2	248	2	Military_img 2	232	6
Barbara	232	6	Medical_img 3	236	5	Military_img 3	244	3
Barche	248	2	Medical_img 4	228	7	Military_img 4	248	2
Plane	252	1	Medical_img 5	244	3	Military_img 5	252	1
Goldhill	244	3	Medical_img 6	256	0	Military_img 6	240	4

Celik et al.'s algorithm

Image	No. of 32 × 64 Unit Blocks	No. of 64 × 128 Merged Blocks	Image	No. of 32 × 64 Unit Blocks	No. of 64 × 128 Merged Blocks	Image	No. of 32 × 64 Unit Blocks	No. of 64 × 128 Merged Blocks
Lena	116	3	Medical_img 1	128	0	Military_img 1	120	2
Mandrill	108	5	Medical_img 2	128	0	Military_img 2	128	0
Barbara	112	4	Medical_img 3	116	3	Military_img 3	124	1
Barche	120	2	Medical_img 4	128	0	Military_img 4	128	0
Plane	124	1	Medical_img 5	124	1	Military_img 5	116	3
Goldhill	120	2	Medical_img 6	120	2	Military_img 6	120	2

(continued)

In this chapter, we present the results of tamper localization by the proposed method for different reversible watermarking algorithms applied to *Military_img 6*. We have reversibly watermarked *Military_img 6* using different reversible watermarking algorithms, and intentionally induced tampering into some of its pixels. The positions of tampering done in the experiment, is shown in

TABLE 6.1: *(continued)*

Ni et al.'s algorithm								
Image	No. of 32 × 64 Unit Blocks	No. of 64 × 128 Merged Blocks	Image	No. of 32 × 64 Unit Blocks	No. of 64 × 128 Merged Blocks	Image	No. of 32 × 64 Unit Blocks	No. of 64 × 128 Merged Blocks
Lena	112	4	Medical_img 1	112	4	Military_img 1	108	5
Mandrill	104	6	Medical_img 2	120	2	Military_img 2	116	3
Barbara	104	6	Medical_img 3	120	2	Military_img 3	104	6
Barche	108	5	Medical_img 4	116	3	Military_img 4	112	4
Plane	116	3	Medical_img 5	112	4	Military_img 5	112	4
Goldhill	116	3	Medical_img 6	120	2	Military_img 6	116	3

Luo et al.'s algorithm								
Image	No. of 32 × 32 Unit Blocks	No. of 64 × 64 Merged Blocks	Image	No. of 32 × 32 Unit Blocks	No. of 64 × 64 Merged Blocks	Image	No. of 32 × 32 Unit Blocks	No. of 64 × 64 Merged Blocks
Lena	248	2	Medical_img 1	248	2	Military_img 1	248	2
Mandrill	240	4	Medical_img 2	256	0	Military_img 2	252	1
Barbara	228	7	Medical_img 3	256	0	Military_img 3	244	3
Barche	248	2	Medical_img 4	252	1	Military_img 4	248	2
Plane	256	0	Medical_img 5	248	2	Military_img 5	248	2
Goldhill	252	1	Medical_img 6	256	0	Military_img 6	252	1

Yang et al.'s algorithm								
Image	No. of 32 × 32 Unit Blocks	No. of 64 × 64 Merged Blocks	Image	No. of 32 × 32 Unit Blocks	No. of 64 × 64 Merged Blocks	Image	No. of 32 × 32 Unit Blocks	No. of 64 × 64 Merged Blocks
Lena	236	5	Medical_img 1	240	4	Military_img 1	240	4
Mandrill	220	9	Medical_img 2	232	6	Military_img 2	236	5
Barbara	224	8	Medical_img 3	240	4	Military_img 3	236	5
Barche	228	7	Medical_img 4	236	5	Military_img 4	228	7
Plane	244	3	Medical_img 5	236	5	Military_img 5	244	3
Goldhill	236	5	Medical_img 6	228	7	Military_img 6	224	8

Fig. 6.4. The results of tamper localization for a particular test image, using different reversible watermarking algorithms, vary according to the tamper localization unit block size determined by Eq. (6.3), as well as the positions of unit blocks and merged blocks, which is determined by the variation in embedding capacity from region to region of the image. The results of tamper local-

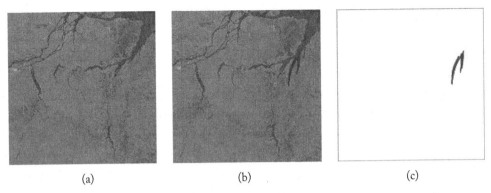

(a)   (b)   (c)

FIGURE 6.4: Intentional tampering induced in the 512×512 *Military_img 6* test image. (a) Reversibly watermarked *Military_img 6*; (b) Tampered, reversibly watermarked *Military_img 6* image; and (c) Positions of tampering in the reversibly watermarked *Military_img 6* image.

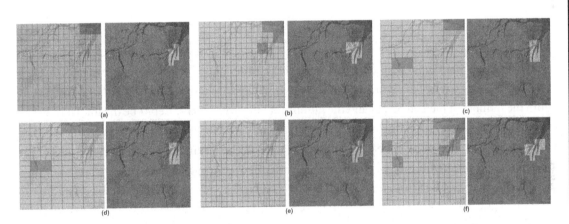

FIGURE 6.5: Tamper localization in reversibly watermarked 512×512 *Military_img 6* image. (*left*) Image divided into tamper localization blocks. Merged blocks are shown in a darker shade. (*right*) Tampered blocks detected. Reversible watermarking algorithms used: (a) Hu et al.'s algorithm [7]; (b) Tian's algorithm [4]; (c) Celik et al.'s algorithm [14]; (d) Ni et al.'s algorithm [20]; (e) Luo et al.'s algorithm [5]; and (f) Yang et al.'s algorithm [6].

ization in *Military_img 6* for different reversible watermarking algorithms are presented in Fig. 6.5. The figures show the tamper localization blocks of the 512×512 *Military_img 6* as well as the final tamper detection and localization achieved by application of the proposed method.

6.5.1 ROBUSTNESS AGAINST FALSE REJECTION

For tamper localization in a reversible watermarking algorithm by the proposed scheme, some of the unit blocks are merged together due to the storage requirement of cover image retrieval information and as well as embedding capacity constraints, as discussed in Section 6.4.1. This causes some non-tampered unit blocks, adjacent to and merged with the actually tampered unit blocks in an image, to get falsely rejected after watermark extraction and authentication (false block rejection was discussed previously in Section 6.4.3). The number of falsely rejected unit blocks, N_f, is given by the following relation:

$$N_f = N_d - T, \tag{6.6}$$

where N_d is the number of tamper localization unit blocks detected to be tampered at the receiver side by the proposed method; and T is the number of unit blocks actually tampered in the reversibly watermarked cover image, at the sender side. The False (block) Rejection Rate (FRR) of an image is calculated as:

$$\text{FRR} = \frac{N_f}{N} \times 100\%. \tag{6.7}$$

where N represents the total number of tamper localization unit blocks in a cover image.

Next, we present a mathematical model to find a closed form solution for FRR as a function of both the number of merged blocks and the number of tampered blocks. Let M be the total number of merged blocks in the image. In our experiments, each merged block was formed by merging together four unit blocks. Therefore, for each unit block tampered, the maximum number of unit blocks that may be falsely rejected is three. Hence, for a particular cover image, the maximum number of unit blocks that may be falsely rejected is given by $3M$. The maximum number of false rejections occurs in an image when each merged block contains one and only one tampered unit block. Hence, the maximum FRR value is given by:

$$\text{FRR}_{max} = \frac{3M}{N} \times 100\%. \tag{6.8}$$

Next, to find an upper bound to the average value of FRR, we must assume that the T tampered unit blocks are uniformly distributed among the M merged blocks, as long as $T \leq 4M$. According to our assumption, whenever $T > 4M$, exactly $(T - 4M)$ tampered blocks must come from the set of unmerged unit blocks. When $T \leq M$, one merged block is rejected per tampered unit block; that is three unit blocks are falsely rejected per tampered unit block. When T varies from $M + 1$ to $4M$, the number of rejected merged blocks remains M, and the number of falsely rejected unit blocks decreases by one from $3M$ with each increase in the value of T by one. When $T > 4M$, according to our assumption, we select the first $4M$ tampered unit blocks from the set of merged blocks leading to zero false rejection. The rest $(T - 4M)$ tampered blocks coming from the set of unmerged unit blocks, again cause zero distortion. Thus, as T varies from 0 to N the number of falsely rejected blocks is given by:

$$
N_f = \begin{cases} 3T & \text{for } 0 \leq T \leq M \\ 4M - T & \text{for } M + 1 \leq T \leq 4M \\ 0 & \text{otherwise.} \end{cases} \tag{6.9}
$$

And an upper bound to the average FRR value, is given by:

$$
\text{FRR}_{avg} = \frac{\left(\sum_{i=0}^{M} 3i + \sum_{i=M+1}^{4M} (4M - i) + \sum_{i=4M+1}^{N} 0 \right)}{(N + 1) \times N} \times 100\%. \tag{6.10}
$$

The minimum value of FRR is always $\text{FRR}_{min} = 0\%$ and this condition occurs whenever all or none of the image blocks are tampered. Note that the above mathematical model derives a theoretic upper bound to the FRR values; therefore, any value of FRR derived through simulations will always be less than or equal to the corresponding theoretic values derived by the model.

Table 6.2 presents the average and maximum FRR derived by the above mathematical model for 18 different test images, watermarked with six different reversible watermarking algorithms [4, 5, 6, 7, 14, 20]. It is evident from our results presented in Tables 6.1 and 6.2, that lower the number of merged blocks in an image, lower is its FRR and for all test images with zero merged blocks, the FRR is always 0%.

We carried out an experiment to find the average FRR over the 18 test images of Fig. 6.2, corresponding to each of the six reversible watermarking algorithms. The unit blocks to be tampered were selected randomly from the entire cover image. At the receiver side, the proposed tamper localization scheme was applied and the number of falsely rejected unit blocks was found out. The empirical results averaged over all 18 test images are presented in Fig. 6.6, which presents the variation of average FRR with varying percentage of tampered unit blocks. It is evident from Fig. 6.6 that the robustness of the proposed method is considerably high since the average FRR for all reversible watermarking algorithms varies between 0% to only 3.1378%. This proves that the tamper localization accuracy of the proposed method is considerably high.

6.5.2 WATERMARK TRANSPARENCY AND EMBEDDING CAPACITY RESULTS

Now we present the watermark transparency results achieved by the proposed method. Since we deal with the class of invisible watermarking (the class of digital watermarking where the watermark,

TABLE 6.2: False rejection rate (FRR) (%) for different test images

Hu et al.'s algorithm								
Image	Average FRR	Maximum FRR	Image	Average FRR	Maximum FRR	Image	Average FRR	Maximum FRR
Lena	0.0091	1.1719	Medical_img 1	0	0	Military_img 1	0	0
Mandrill	0.7387	10.5469	Medical_img 2	0	0	Military_img 2	0	0
Barbara	2.0519	17.5781	Medical_img 3	0	0	Military_img 3	0.0091	1.1719
Barche	0	0	Medical_img 4	0.0821	3.5156	Military_img 4	0.0365	2.3438
Plane	0	0	Medical_img 5	0	0	Military_img 5	0	0
Goldhill	0	0	Medical_img 6	0.0821	3.5156	Military_img 6	0.0365	2.3438

Tian's algorithm								
Image	Average FRR	Maximum FRR	Image	Average FRR	Maximum FRR	Image	Average FRR	Maximum FRR
Lena	0.0365	2.3438	Medical_img 1	0.0091	1.1719	Military_img 1	0.1459	4.6875
Mandrill	1.7875	16.4063	Medical_img 2	0.0365	2.3438	Military_img 2	0.3283	7.0313
Barbara	0.3283	7.0313	Medical_img 3	0.2280	5.8594	Military_img 3	0.0821	3.5156
Barche	0.0365	2.3438	Medical_img 4	0.4469	8.2031	Military_img 4	0.0365	2.3438
Plane	0.0091	1.1719	Medical_img 5	0.0821	3.5156	Military_img 5	0.0091	1.1719
Goldhill	0.0821	3.5156	Medical_img 6	0	0	Military_img 6	0.1459	4.6875

Celik et al.'s algorithm								
Image	Average FRR	Maximum FRR	Image	Average FRR	Maximum FRR	Image	Average FRR	Maximum FRR
Lena	0.3270	7.0313	Medical_img 1	0	0	Military_img 1	0.1453	4.6875
Mandrill	0.9084	11.7188	Medical_img 2	0	0	Military_img 2	0	0
Barbara	0.5814	9.3750	Medical_img 3	0.3270	7.0313	Military_img 3	0.0363	2.3438
Barche	0.1453	4.6875	Medical_img 4	0	0	Military_img 4	0	0
Plane	0.0363	2.3438	Medical_img 5	0.0363	2.3438	Military_img 5	0.3270	7.0313
Goldhill	0.1453	4.6875	Medical_img 6	0.1453	4.6875	Military_img 6	0.1453	4.6875

embedded into the cover image, is imperceptible to the human visual system) in this book, the distortion produced in the cover image due to watermarking is desirably minimal. We have measured the distortion of the cover images in terms of *Peak Signal to Noise Ratio* (PSNR) [1].

Table 6.3 presents the test image distortions, along with the size of pure watermark embedded by the application of the proposed method to Hu et al.'s scheme. (Hu et al.'s scheme is chosen to report the results in Table 6.3, since Hu et al.'s Difference Expansion-based Reversible Watermarking Algorithm [7] produces the best quality watermarked images after application of the proposed tamper localization method; this is also supported by our comparison results presented in Table 6.4.)

TABLE 6.2: *(continued)*

				Ni et al.'s algorithm				
Image	Average FRR	Maximum FRR	Image	Average FRR	Maximum FRR	Image	Average FRR	Maximum FRR
Lena	0.5814	9.3750	Medical_img 1	0.5814	9.3750	Military_img 1	0.9084	11.7188
Mandrill	1.3081	14.0625	Medical_img 2	0.1453	4.6875	Military_img 2	0.3270	7.0313
Barbara	1.3081	14.0625	Medical_img 3	0.1453	4.6875	Military_img 3	1.3081	14.0625
Barche	0.9084	11.7188	Medical_img 4	0.3270	7.0313	Military_img 4	0.5814	9.3750
Plane	0.3270	7.0313	Medical_img 5	0.5814	9.3750	Military_img 5	0.5814	9.3750
Goldhill	0.3270	7.0313	Medical_img 6	0.1453	4.6875	Military_img 6	0.3270	7.0313

				Luo et al.'s algorithm				
Image	Average FRR	Maximum FRR	Image	Average FRR	Maximum FRR	Image	Average FRR	Maximum FRR
Lena	0.0365	2.3438	Medical_img 1	0.0365	2.3438	Military_img 1	0.0365	2.3438
Mandrill	0.1459	4.6875	Medical_img 2	0	0	Military_img 2	0.0091	1.1719
Barbara	0.4469	8.2031	Medical_img 3	0	0	Military_img 3	0.0821	3.5156
Barche	0.0365	2.3438	Medical_img 4	0.0091	1.1719	Military_img 4	0.0365	2.3438
Plane	0	0	Medical_img 5	0.0365	2.3438	Military_img 5	0.0365	2.3438
Goldhill	0.0091	1.1719	Medical_img 6	0	0	Military_img 6	0.0091	1.1719

				Yang et al.'s algorithm				
Image	Average FRR	Maximum FRR	Image	Average FRR	Maximum FRR	Image	Average FRR	Maximum FRR
Lena	0.2280	5.8594	Medical_img 1	0.1459	4.6875	Military_img 1	0.1459	4.6875
Mandrill	0.7387	10.5469	Medical_img 2	0.3283	7.0313	Military_img 2	0.2280	5.8594
Barbara	0.5837	9.3750	Medical_img 3	0.1459	4.6875	Military_img 3	0.2280	5.8594
Barche	0.4469	8.2031	Medical_img 4	0.2280	5.8594	Military_img 4	0.4469	8.2031
Plane	0.0821	3.5156	Medical_img 5	0.2280	5.8594	Military_img 5	0.0821	3.5156
Goldhill	0.2280	5.8594	Medical_img 6	0.4469	8.2031	Military_img 6	0.5837	9.3750

Pure watermark does not include any cover image retrieval information, such as the block identification bits or the block retrieval information which are embedded into the cover image. Table 6.3 presents the PSNR of a cover image in terms of dB, and its embedded watermark size in terms of bits-per-pixel (bpp). Also, the cover image distortion results for the test images *Mandri ll*, *Medical_img 1* and *Military_img 1* are shown in Fig. 6.7.

In this chapter we compared the quality of the watermarked images produced by our proposed scheme with those produced by other state-of-the-art reversible watermarking schemes having authentication capabilities. The other schemes used in our comparison are those proposed by Yan et

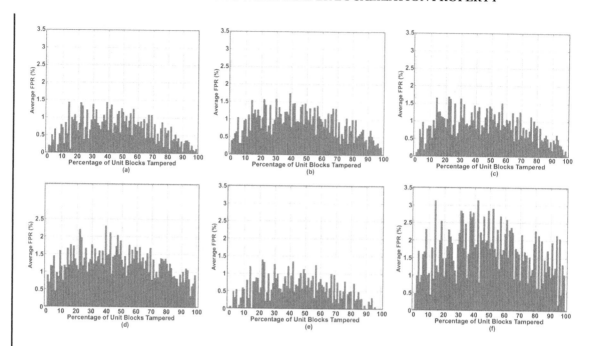

FIGURE 6.6: Average False Rejection Rate (FRR) of the proposed scheme vs. percentage of tampered unit blocks. Average taken over all 18 test images. Reversible watermarking algorithms used: (a) Hu et al.'s algorithm [7]; (b) Tian's algorithm [4]; (c) Celik et al.'s algorithm [14]; (d) Ni et al.'s algorithm [20]; (e) Luo et al.'s algorithm [5]; and (f) Yang et al.'s algorithm [6].

TABLE 6.3: Distortion (PSNR) produced in different test images by the proposed method

512×512 Standard Test Images			512×512 Medical Test Images			512×512 Military Test Images		
Image	Watermark (bpp)	PSNR (dB)	Image	Watermark (bpp)	PSNR (dB)	Image	Watermark (bpp)	PSNR (dB)
Lena	0.1235	55.0864	Medical_img 1	0.1250	41.6747	Military_img 1	0.1250	41.2483
Mandrill	0.1118	41.4255	Medical_img 2	0.1250	41.7235	Military_img 2	0.1250	42.0634
Barbara	0.1030	41.5058	Medical_img 3	0.1250	64.3315	Military_img 3	0.1235	41.7730
Barche	0.1250	52.6493	Medical_img 4	0.1206	46.7947	Military_img 4	0.1221	41.2597
Plane	0.1250	54.7068	Medical_img 5	0.1250	41.1421	Military_img 5	0.1250	41.8912
Goldhill	0.1250	50.3966	Medical_img 6	0.1206	58.8298	Military_img 6	0.1221	42.0234

TABLE 6.4: Distortion (PSNR) comparison results for 512 × 512 *Lena* image

Schemes	PSNR (dB)	Pure Watermark (bits)
Proposed scheme applied to Hu et al.'s algorithm [7]	52.5	51,500
Proposed scheme applied to Tian's algorithm [4]	51.87	51,500
Proposed scheme applied to Celik et al.'s algorithm [14]	51.67	51,500
Proposed scheme applied to Ni et al.'s algorithm [20]	54.73	5,500
Proposed scheme applied to Luo et al.'s algorithm [5]	52.38	51,500
Proposed scheme applied to Yang et al.'s algorithm [6]	50.5	51,500
Yan et al.'s [70] scheme	49.4	51,430
Wu's [71] scheme	43.4	5,460
Lee et al.'s [57] scheme	52.2	26,990
Bausys et al.'s [72] scheme	37.8	5,460

(a) Mandrill   (b) Medical_img 1   (c) Military_img 1

FIGURE 6.7: Cover image distortions produced by the proposed method. (*left*) Original image; (*right*) Watermarked image.

al. [70], Wu [71], Lee et al. [57] and Bausys et al. [72]. The comparison results for the 512 × 512 *Lena* image are presented in Table 6.4, where we have reported the comparison results pertaining to the application of the proposed method to six different reversible watermarking algorithms. Note here that among the other schemes used for comparison, Yan et al.'s [70] scheme has embedded the maximum sized payload with 51,430 bits. Hence for the sake of fair comparison, we embedded 51, 500 bits of pure watermark into the 512 × 512 *Lena* image wherever possible. However, due to limitation of the maximum embedding capacity offered by Ni et al.'s [20] algorithm, in this case we have embedded only 5, 500 bits of pure watermark.

It is evident from our experimental results presented in Tables 6.3 and 6.4 that the watermarked image quality achieved by the proposed method is considerably high compared to the state-of-the-art. This is due to the fact that by the proposed method, additional cover image re-trieval information is required only for the merged blocks of the cover image, as described in detail in Section 6.4.1. For rest of the blocks not even a single bit of additional information is needed; they embed only pure watermark/hash bits. Thus embedding the same size of pure watermark by the proposed method into a particular image, produces much lesser distortion compared to other state-of-the-art schemes, which generally need to embed cover image retrieval information for the *entire* image, in addition to the pure watermark/hash bits. This property of the proposed scheme also helps to maximize its pure watermark embedding capacity.

6.6   SUMMARY

Reversible watermarking algorithms are typically *fragile*, and hence vulnerable to trivial tampering attacks by adversaries, as well as rejection of the received image because of uncorrectable pixel values. In situations where repeated retransmission of data is not feasible, this effectively results in a DoS form of attack. In this chapter, we presented a tamper localization technique for reversibly watermarked grayscale images based on the optimal expansion of tampered pixel blocks. This algorithm has high tamper detection resolution, thus resulting in minimal rejection of non-tampered pixels. The algorithm also helps to minimize the retrieval information requirement of reversible watermarking algorithms, hence maximizing the pure watermark embedding capacity, as is evident from Section 6.5. It also minimizes the *False Rejection Rate* of cover image pixels, in case of authentication failure at the receiver side. Thus, the technique helps to overcome the two major challenges of reversible watermarking discussed in Chapter 5.

In our experimental results in Section 6.5, we showed the minimum block size large enough to embed a 128-bit MD5 hash; however, both the hash size as well as the block size may be varied according to the user's requirements. In order to embed any additional information into the cover data, we would select a larger block size to have enough embedding space (to embed that information in addition to the authentication information).

CHAPTER 7

Looking Forward

With the worldwide proliferation of the internet in recent years, multimedia content protection has become a critical concern for computer scientists and researchers worldwide. *Digital watermarking* is a widely adopted technology for protection, authentication and authorization of digital multimedia data against various security threats. *Reversible watermarking*, in addition to solving the purpose of multimedia content protection, also achieves lossless recovery from distortion inherently induced by digital watermarking of multimedia data.

The area of reversible watermarking has rapidly gained extensive research interest in the recent years. In this book, we focused on reversible watermarking of digital images. We presented case studies in Chapter 2, on the necessity and motivation behind research on reversible watermarking. We also studied the operating principles of various classes of reversible watermarking algorithms in Chapter 3, along a very recently proposed technique for reversible watermarking of digital grayscale images. We also described a software platform to evaluate and compare several reversible watermarking algorithms. The present challenges of design and implementation of reversible watermarking algorithms, as discussed in Chapter 5, pave the direction for future research in this field.

Evaluation of reversible watermarking algorithms proves to be highly resources intensive, given the fact that such algorithms are highly computationally involved, with complex mathematical steps constituting their major building blocks. In such a scenario, a useful tool would be a framework to analyze the operation of those algorithms theoretically, and estimate their performance, thus avoiding the resource requirements for actual implementation. To the best of our knowledge, the current state-of-the-art lacks such a theoretic model. Other major directions for future research on this topic include the development of an information theory-based framework to estimate performances of such algorithms a priori, for comparison between various classes of reversible watermarking algorithms. Such a theoretical framework would complement the software framework described in Chapter 3.

Due to complex mathematical operations involved in the implementation of reversible watermarking algorithms, such algorithms have considerably large runtime requirements compared to their non-reversible counterparts, and the reduction in runtime is a major challenge of design and implementation of reversible watermarking algorithms. Many reversible watermarking algorithms have are block-based [6], and hence amenable to improvement in runtime through parallelization. Hardware accelerators are also promising in this regard.

Bibliography

[1] I. J. Cox, M. L. Miller, J. A. Bloom, J. Fridrich, and T. Kalker, *Digital Watermarking and Steganography*. Morgan Kaufmann Publishers, 2008. 1, 2, 8, 92

[2] C. Conrado and M. Petkovic and Veen, M. V. D. and Velde, W. V. D., "Controlled sharing of personal content using digital rights management," in *E. Fernández-Medina (Ed.), Proc. of the 4th International Workshop on Security in Information Systems (WOSIS)*, pp. 173–185, 2005. DOI: 10.1.1.89.1010. 1

[3] International Business Machines Corporation. Research Division and L. C. Anderson and J. B. Lotspiech, "Rights Management and Security in the Electronic Library," *IBM Research Division*, 1995. DOI: 10.1002/bult.8. 1

[4] J. Tian, "Reversible data embedding using a difference expansion," *IEEE Transactions on Circuits Systems and Video Technology*, vol. 13, pp. 890–896, Aug. 2003. DOI: 10.1109/TCSVT.2003.815962. 3, 25, 28, 63, 64, 73, 74, 75, 76, 85, 86, 89, 91, 94, 95

[5] L. Luo, Z. Chen, M. Chen, X. Zeng, and Z. Xiong, "Reversible image watermarking using interpolation technique," *IEEE Transactions on Information Forensics and Security*, vol. 5, pp. 187–193, Mar. 2010. DOI: 10.1109/TIFS.2009.2035975. 3, 9, 11, 13, 15, 25, 37, 38, 63, 74, 76, 86, 89, 91, 94, 95

[6] B. Yang, M. Schmucker, W. Funk, C. Busch, and S. Sun, "Integer DCT–based reversible watermarking technique for images using companding technique," in *Proceedings of SPIE*, vol. 5306, pp. 405–415, 2004. DOI: 10.1117/12.527216. 3, 26, 43, 63, 66, 74, 75, 76, 86, 89, 91, 94, 95, 98

[7] Y. Hu, H. K. Lee, and J. Li, "DE–based reversible data hiding with improved overflow location map," *IEEE Transactions on Circuits Systems and Video Technology*, vol. 19, pp. 250–260, Feb. 2009. DOI: 10.1109/TCSVT.2008.2009252. 3, 74, 78, 79, 80, 85, 86, 89, 91, 92, 94, 95

[8] J. B. Feng, I. C. Lin, C. S. Tsai, and Y. P. Chu, "Reversible watermarking: Current status and key issues," *International Journal of Network Security*, vol. 2, pp. 161–171, May 2006. DOI: 10.1.1.97.507. 27, 73, 85

[9] K. S. Kim, M. J. Lee, H. Y.Lee, and H. K. Lee, "Reversible data hiding exploiting spatial correlation between sub-sampled images," *Pattern Recognition*, vol. 42, pp. 3083–3096, 2009. DOI: 10.1016/j.patcog.2009.04.004. 37

[10] J. Tian, "Reversible watermarking by difference expansion," in *Proceedings of Workshop on Multimedia and Security*, pp. 19–22, Dec. 2002. 25, 28

[11] S. Weng, Y. Zhao, J. S. Pan, and R. Ni, "A novel reversible watermarking based on an integer transform," *Proceedings of International Conference on Image Processing*, pp. 241–244, Sep. 2007. DOI: 10.1109/ICIP.2007.4379291. 25, 28, 63, 75, 76

[12] H. J. Kim, V. Sachnev, Y. Q. Shi, J. Nam, and H. G. Choo, "A novel difference expansion transform for reversible data embedding," *IEEE Transactions on Information Forensics and Security*, vol. 3, pp. 456–465, Aug. 2008. DOI: 10.1109/TIFS.2008.924600. 28

[13] P. Howard, F. Kossentini, and B. Martins, "The emerging jbig2 standard," *IEEE Transactions on Circuits and Systems for Video Technology*, vol. 8, pp. 338–348, Sep. 1998. DOI: 10.1109/76.735380. 28

[14] M. U. Celik, G. Sharma, A. M. Tekalp, and E. Saber, "Lossless generalized-lsb data embedding," *IEEE Transactions on Image Processing*, vol. 14, pp. 253–266, Feb. 2005. DOI: 10.1109/TIP.2004.840686. 3, 25, 31, 74, 85, 86, 89, 91, 94, 95

[15] M. Celik, G. Sharma, A. Tekalp, and E. Saber, "Localized lossless authentication watermark (law)," *International Society for Optical Engineering*, vol. 5020, pp. 689–698, Jan. 2003. DOI: 10.1117/12.477312. 31

[16] M. Celik, G. Sharma, A. Tekalp, and E. Saber, "Reversible data hiding," in *Proceedings of International Conference on Image Processing*, pp. III–157–III–160, Sep. 2002. DOI: 10.1109/ICIP.2002.1039911. 25, 31

[17] J. Fridrich, M. Goljan, and R. Du, "Lossless data embedding—new paradigm in digital watermarking," *EURASIP Journal of Signal Processing*, vol. 2002, pp. 185–196, Feb. 2002. DOI: 10.1155/S1110865702000537. 31

[18] J. Fridrich, M. Goljan, and R. Du, "Distortion free data embedding," *Proceedings of 4th Information Hiding Workshop*, vol. 2137, pp. 27–41, Apr. 2001. DOI: 10.1007/3-540-45496-9_3. 31

[19] V. Bhaskaran and K. Konstantinides, *Image and Video Compression Standards: Algorithms and Applications*. 2nd ed. Norwell, MA: Kluwer, 1995. DOI: 10.1007/978-1-4757-2358-8. 31, 66, 82

[20] Z. Ni, Y. Q. Shi, N. Ansari, and W. Su, "Reversible data hiding," *IEEE Transactions on Circuits and Systems for Video Technology*, vol. 16, pp. 354–362, 2006. DOI: 10.1109/TCSVT.2006.869964. 3, 18, 33, 74, 85, 86, 89, 91, 94, 95

[21] Z. Ni, Y. Shi, N. Ansari, and S. Wei, "Reversible data hiding," *Proceedings of International Symposium on Circuits and Systems*, vol. 2, pp. II–912–II–915, May 2003. DOI: 10.1109/TCSVT.2006.869964. 33

[22] C. D. Vleeschouwer, J. F. Delaigle, and B. Macq, "Circular interpretation of histogram for reversible watermarking," in *Proceedings of the IEEE 4th Workshop on Multimedia Signal Processing*, pp. 345–350, Oct. 2001. DOI: 10.1109/MMSP.2001.962758. 33, 36

[23] C. D. Vleeschouwer, J. Delaigle, and B. Mac, "Circular interpretation of bijective transformations in lossless watermarking for media asset management," *IEEE Transactions on Multimedia*, vol. 5, pp. 97–105, Mar. 2003. DOI: 10.1109/TMM.2003.809729. 33, 36

[24] X. Li, W. Zhang, X. Gui, and B. Yang, "A Novel Reversible Data Hiding Scheme Based on Two-Dimensional Difference–Histogram Modification," *IEEE Transactions on Information Forensics and Security*, vol. 8, pp. 1091–1100, Jul. 2013. DOI: 10.1109/TIFS.2013.2261062. 40

[25] R. Naskar and R. S. Chakraborty, "Reversible watermarking utilizing weighted-median based prediction," *IET Image Processing*, vol. 6, pp. 507–520, Jul. 2012. DOI: 10.1049/iet-ipr.2011.0244. 37, 47

[26] R. Naskar and R. S. Chakraborty, "Reversible image watermarking through coordinate logic operation based prediction," in *In Proceedings of 7th International Conference of Information System Security (ICISS 11)*, LNCS 7093, pp. 190–203, Dec. 2011. DOI: 10.1007/978-3-642-25560-1_13. 37

[27] R. Naskar and R. S. Chakraborty, "Reversible image watermarking through coordinate logic operation based prediction," in *In Proceedings of 8th International Conference of Information System Security (ICISS 12)*, LNCS 7671, pp. 149–163, Dec. 2012. 37

[28] G. Plonka and M. Tasche, "Integer DCT-ii by lifting steps," *International Series in Numerical Mathematics*, vol. 145, pp. 235–252, 2003. DOI: 10.1.1.57.7363. 43

[29] B. Stanberry, "Legal ethical and risk issues in telemedicine," *Comp. Meth. Prog. Biomed.*, vol. 64, pp. 225–233, Mar. 2001. DOI: 10.1016/S0169-2607(00)00142-5. 7

[30] T. Eid, "Action report," *Western Governors Association 1995*, pp. 42–47, Jun. 1995. 7

[31] R. Velumani and V. Seenivasagam, "A reversible blind medical image watermarking scheme for patient identification, improved telediagnosis and tamper detection with a facial image watermark," *2010 IEEE International Conference on Computational Intelligence and Computing Research (ICCIC)*, pp. 1–8, Dec. 2010. DOI: 10.1109/ICCIC.2010.5705832. 8

[32] S. Berger and B. Cepelewicz, "Medical-legal issues in teleradiology," *American Journal of Roentgenol*, vol. 166, pp. 505–510, Mar. 1996. DOI: 10.2214/ajr.166.3.8623616.

[33] S. Raviraja, S. Osman, and Kardman, "A novel technique for malaria diagnosis using invariant moments and by image compression," *IFMBE Proceedings 2008*, vol. 21, pp. 730–733, Jun. 2008. DOI: 10.1007/978-3-540-69139-6_182. 8

[34] R. Wang, C. Lin, and J. Lin, "Microscopic determination of malaria parasite load: role of image analysis," *Microscopy: Science, Technology, Application and Education, FORMATEX 2010*, vol. 3, pp. 862–866, 2010. 8

[35] G. Diaz, F. Gonzalez, and E. Romero, "A semi automatic method for quantification and classification of erythrocytes infected with malaria parasites in microscopic image," *Journal of Biomedical Informatics*, vol. 42, pp. 296–307, Apr. 2009. DOI: 10.1016/j.jbi.2008.11.005. 9

[36] F. Tek, A. Dempster, and I. Kale, "Malaria parasite detection in peripheral blood images," in *Proceedings of British machine vision conference*, Sep. 2006. DOI: 10.1.1.138.5356. 9

[37] S. Toha and U. Ngah, "Computer aided medical diagnosis for the identification of malaria parasites," in *IEEE ICSCN 2007*, pp. 521–522, Feb. 2007. DOI: 10.1109/ICSCN.2007.350655. 9

[38] N. Ross, C. Pritchard, and D. Rubin, "Automatic image processing method for the diagnosis and classification of malaria on thin blood smears," *Med. Biol. Eng. Comput.*, vol. 44, pp. 427–436, Apr. 2006. DOI: http://dx.doi.org/10.1007/s11517-006-0044-2. 9

[39] V. Makkapati and R. Rao, "Segmentation on malaria parasites in peripheral blood smear images," in *IEEE International conference on acoustics, speech and signal processing*, pp. 1361–1364, Apr. 2009. DOI: 10.1109/ICASSP.2009.4959845. 9

[40] Dempster and C. Ruberto, "Morphological processing of malarial slide images," in *Matlab DSP Conference*, Nov. 1999. 9

[41] R. Naskar and R. S. Chakraborty, "Reversible Watermarking: Theory and Practice," Dr. B. Issac (ed.), *Case Studies in Secure Computing—Achievements and Trends*. CRC Press, 2001.

[42] D. Das, M. Ghosh, C. Chakraborty, A. K. Maiti, and M. Pal, "Probabilistic prediction of malaria using morphological and textural information," in *Proceedings of International Conference on Image Information Processing (ICIIP) 2011*, Nov. 2011. DOI: 10.1109/ICIIP.2011.6108879. 9

[43] R. Wang, C. Lin, and J. Lin, "Image hiding by optimal lsb substitution and genetic algorithm," *Pattern Recognition*, vol. 34, pp. 671–683, Dec. 2000. DOI: 10.1016/S0031-3203(00)00015-7. 9, 11

[44] S. Mitra and J. Sicuranza, *Nonlinear Image Processing*. San Diego: Academic Press, 2001. 10

[45] N. Otsu, "A threshold selection method from gray-level histograms," *IEEE Transactions on Systems, Man and Cybernetics*, vol. 9, pp. 62–66, Jan. 1979. DOI: 10.1109/TSMC.1979.4310076. 10

[46] R. Gonzalez and R. Woods, *Digital Image Processing*. 2002. 11

[47] R. Haralick and S. Sternberg, "Image analysis using mathematical morphology," *IEEE Transactions on Pattern Analysis and Machine Intelligence*, vol. 9, pp. 532–550, Jul. 1987. DOI: 10.1109/TPAMI.1987.4767941. 11, 12

[48] R. Wang, C. Lin, and J. Lin, *Fundamentals of Biostatistics*. Ane Books, India, 2008. 11, 12

[49] D. Scott, *Multivariate Density Estimation*. Wiley, 1992. DOI: 10.1002/9780470316849. 13

[50] Playboy Magazine, "Lena Image," Nov 1972. 56

[51] CVG–UGR Image Database *Computer Vision Group, University of Granada*, http://decsai.ugr.es/cvg/dbimagenes/. 56

[52] S. P. Maity and S. Maity, "Multistage spread spectrum watermark detection technique using fuzzy logic," *IEEE Signal Processing Letters*, vol. 16, pp. 245–248, Apr. 2009. DOI: 10.1109/LSP.2009.2014097.

[53] S. C. Tamane, R. R. Manza, and R. R. Deshmukh, "3d models watermarking using fuzzy logic," in *IEEE 2009 International Conference on Advances in Computing, Control and Telecommunication Technologies*, pp. 195–197, Dec. 2009. DOI: 10.1109/ACT.2009.56.

[54] S. Queslati, A. Cherif, and B. Solaiman, "A fuzzy watermarking system using the wavelet technique for medical images," *International Journal of Research and Reviews in Computing Engineering*, vol. 1, pp. 43–48, Mar. 2011.

[55] F. Russo, "Recent advances in fuzzy techniques for image enhancement," *IEEE Transactions on Instrumentation and Measurement*, vol. 47, pp. 1428–1434, 1998. DOI: 10.1109/19.746707.

[56] F. Russo, "Fire operators for image processing," *Fuzzy Sets Syst.*, vol. 103, pp. 265–275, 1999. DOI: 10.1016/S0165-0114(98)00226-7.

[57] C. S. Lee and Y. H. Kuo, "Fuzzy techniques in image processing," *Studies in Fuzziness and Soft Computing, ch. Adaptive fuzzy filter and its application to image enhancement, New York: Springer–Verlag*, vol. 52, pp. 172–193, 2000. 73, 74, 95

[58] R. C. Gonzales and R. C. Woods, *Digital Image Processing*. MA: Addison-Wesley, 1992.

[59] C. J. Lin, R. C. Weng, and S. S. Keerthi, "Trust region newton method for large-scale logistic regression," *Journal of Machine Learning Research*, vol. 9, pp. 627–650, Apr. 2008. DOI: 10.1145/1273496.1273567.

[60] M. Abramowitz and I. A. Stegun (eds.), *Handbook of Mathematical Functions*. National Bureau of Standards, Applied Mathematics Series, 1965.

[61] T. H. Crystal, A. S. Nielsen, and E. Marsh, "Speech in noisy environments (SPINE) adds new dimension to speech recognition R&D," in *Proceedings of the Second International Conference on Human Language Technology Research*, pp. 212–216, 2002. DOI: 10.3115/1289189.1289199. 17, 25, 65

[62] M. Suite, H. R. Burris, C. I. Moore, M. F. Stell, L. Wasiczko, W. Freeman, W. S. Rabinovich, G. C. Gilbreath, and W. J. Scharp, "Packet testing in free-space optical communication links over water," in *Proceedings of SPIE*, 6215, pp. 621505-1–621505-10, 2006. DOI: 10.1117/12.668128. 17, 25

[63] A. Reed and J. N. Hopkinson, *Data Transmission System with Automatic Repeat Request*. U.S. Patent No. 4939731, 1990. 17, 25, 65

[64] R. Singh, M. L. Seltzer, B. Raj, and R. M. Stern, "Speech in noisy environments: robust automatic segmentation, feature extraction, and hypothesis combination," in *Proceedings of IEEE Conference on Acoustics, Speech and Signal Processing*, pp. 273–276, May 2001. 17, 25, 65

[65] S. Lin and D. J. Costello, *Error Control Coding (2nd edition)*. Prentice Hall, 2004. 19, 20, 79

[66] P. Elias, "Coding for noisy channelss," *IRE Convention Record*, vol. 3, pp. 37–46, Mar. 1995. 25, 65

[67] V. Britanak and K. R. Rao, *Discrete Cosine and Sine Transforms: General Properties, Fast Algorithms and Integer Approximations*. Academic Press, 2006. 26

[68] R. Naskar, and R. S. Chakraborty, "Performance of Reversible Digital Image Watermarking under Error-prone Data Communication: a Simulation-based Study," *IET Image Processing*, vol. 6, no. 6, pp. 728-737, Aug. 2012. DOI: 10.1049/iet-ipr.2011.0160. 18

[69] R. Naskar, and R. S. Chakraborty, "A Generalized Tamper Localization Approach for Reversible Watermarking Algorithms," *ACM Transactions on Multimedia Computing Communications and Applications*, vol. 9, no. 3, article 19, Jun. 2013. DOI: 10.1145/2487268.2487272. 73

[70] Y. Yan, W. Cao, and S. Li, "High capacity reversible image authentication based on difference image watermarking," in *IEEE International Workshop on Imaging Systems and Techniques*, pp. 183–186, May 2009. DOI: 10.1109/IST.2009.5071628. 73, 74, 95

[71] X. Wu, "Reversible semi–fragile watermarking based on histogram shifting of integer wavelet coefficients," in *IEEE Proc. of DEST '07, Inaugural IEEE-IES*, pp. 501–505, Feb. 2007. DOI: 10.1109/DEST.2007.372028. 73, 74, 95

[72] R. Bausys and A. Kriukovas, "Reversible watermarking scheme for image authentication in frequency domain," in *International Symposium ELMAR–2006*, pp. 53–56, Jun. 2006. DOI: 10.1109/ELMAR.2006.329513. 73, 74, 95

[73] H. M. Tsai and L. W. Chang, "Secure reversible visible image watermarking with authentication," *Signal Processing: Image Communication*, vol. 25, pp. 10–17, 2010. DOI: 10.1016/j.image.2009.11.002. 74

[74] N. Wang and C. Men, "Reversible fragile watermarking for 2–D vector map authentication with localization," *Computer-Aided Design*, vol. 44, pp. 320–330, 2012. DOI: 10.1016/j.cad.2011.11.001. 74

[75] R. Rivest, *The MD5 message–digest algorithm*. NetworkWorking Group, Request for Comments (RFC) 1321, Apr 1992. 79, 86

[76] J. Sobolewski, *Cyclic redundancy check*. Encyclopedia of Computer Science, 2003. 79

Authors' Biographies

RUCHIRA NASKAR

Ruchira Naskar received a B.Tech degree in Information Technology from West Bengal University of Technology in 2008, and an M.Tech degree in Information Technology from Indian Institute of Technology, Kharagpur in 2010. Since July 2010, she has been a research scholar in the Department of Computer Science and Engineering at Indian Institute of Technology, Kharagpur. Her research interest is in the areas of digital watermarking, multimedia content protection and cryptography.

Currently she is working as an Assistant Professor at the National Institute of Technology Rourkela, India.

RAJAT SUBHRA CHAKRABORTY

Rajat Subhra Chakraborty has been an Assistant Professor in the Computer Science and Engineering Department of IIT Kharagpur since 2010. He received a Ph.D. in Computer Engineering from Case Western Reserve University (USA) and a B.E. (Hons.) in Electronics and Telecommunication Engineering from Jadavpur University (India) in 2005. His professional experience includes a stint as CAD Software Engineer at National Semiconductor, and a graduate internship at AMD Headquarters at Santa Clara (California). His research interests include Hardware Security including: design methodology for hardware IP/IC protection; Hardware Trojan detection and prevention through design and testing, attacks on hardware implementation of cryptographic algorithms; and reversible watermarking for digital content protection. Dr. Chakraborty has published over 45 articles in international journals and conferences. He has delivered keynote talks and tutorials at several international conferences and workshops, and has rendered his service as a reviewer and program committee member for multiple international conferences and journals. He is the co-author of three book chapters and two forthcoming books and was one of the recipients of the "IBM Faculty Award" for 2012. He holds one US patent, and two more international patents and one Indian patent have been filed based on his research work. Dr. Chakraborty is a member of IEEE and ACM.

Printed in the United States
by Baker & Taylor Publisher Services